S
FOLKLORE

Isobel E. Williams

Chambers

Published 1991 by W & R Chambers Ltd,
43–45 Annandale Street, Edinburgh EH7 4AZ

British Library Cataloguing in Publication Data
Williams, Isobel E.
   Scottish folklore.—(Chambers mini guides)
   1. Scottish folklore
   I. Title
   398.09411

ISBN 0-550-20067-3

The song on p 45 appears by courtesy of
Brian McNeill/Kinmor Music.

Illustrations by John Haxby, Janet MacKay
Cover design by John Marshall

Typeset by Pillans & Wilson Ltd, Edinburgh
Printed in Singapore by
Singapore National Printers Ltd

Introduction

Everyone in Scotland is confronted daily with items of folklore, whether it be the local name for a flower, a building or a football team; in passing one of the many pubs with names evocative of the Jacobite rebellion or some long-forgotten hero; or by some superstitious belief or relic of an old religion. Even in our high-technology age many of us prefer to put our trust in such weatherlore as 'A red sky at night is a shepherd's delight' rather than in the TV weatherman.

The word 'folklore' was coined in 1846 by W.J. Thoms, editor of the *Athenaeum* and founder of *Notes and Queries,* and was used by him to mean 'the traditional beliefs, customs, legends and superstitions of a people'. Common usages, social mores, rites and ceremonies, stories and ballads, proverbs, games, weatherlore and plantlore also come under the heading of folklore; the subject comprises the domestic commonplaces and traditions which, together with history, make up the colourful weave of a national heritage.

The folklore of a country is often intricately bound up with historical facts. Often sharp and critical, folklore provides a good counterbalance to the official version of history. A fact of Scottish life is that for centuries the country and its people have felt under threat from English domination. The Scots language has been relegated to second place in favour of English and, until relatively recently, Scottish history was not taught in Scottish schools. Without wishing to promote any anti-English feeling, no book on Scottish folklore would be complete without its share of anecdotes and songs about the 'Auld Enemy'.

Though the word, the science and a lot of the material is old, folklore is very much alive and growing! Scottish folk-music can be heard daily on the radio or in pubs and folk-clubs throughout the country and a new generation of Scottish singer-songwriters is making itself heard. Many traditional stories have recently been published and the art of story-telling seems at last to be gaining the recognition it deserves, with story-telling workshops, seminars and competitions being held regularly.

There are no 'rights' and 'wrongs' in folklore. Events and stories are embroidered upon in the retelling and the names of towns or people are changed to give a story a more local flavour. The same person can be either hero or villain, depending on who is telling the tale, and genuine mix-ups occur when characters in history have the same name or when one character has more than one name. Dates become similarly confused and the two calendars which were in operation during the first half of the eighteenth century – the old-style Julian Calendar was retained in Great Britain until January 1752, while the Roman Catholic countries had long adopted the Gregorian Calendar – do nothing to help ascertain chronology. In an attempt to untangle some of these problems I have included short explanations of the historical facts behind some of the legends.

Items are listed alphabetically with *italics* used to direct readers to related items.

Folklore is above all a study of what *people* are doing and saying. It is not the received history of kings and queens that is taught at school, but rather the domestic, homely history of a people, handed down, more often than not by word of mouth. Communication is the essence of folklore, talking with people, listening and asking questions and exchanging information. For this reason, I would like to thank the many friends and members of the family who contributed towards this book with items of folklore and with research.

Scottish Folklore

A

Achaius Eighth-century king of the Scots. He is credited with having formed the *Auld Alliance* together with Charlemagne.

Alba One of the names for Scotland, from Celtic *alp* or *ailp* meaning rock or cliff. It is the name most often used in Irish legends to refer to Scotland. Other names for Scotland which come from this root are: Albainn, Albany, Albin, Albion.
  (See *Caledonia, Dalriada, Scotia.)*

Annandale Christians According to *Scott,* a woman went begging in the Border village of Annandale. She was having no luck and so she complained to a local man, asking if there were any Christians in Annandale. The reply was as follows: 'There's nae Christians here . . . we're a' Johnstones and Jardines.'

Antiquary This was a well-respected title in the eighteenth century for a folklorist and collector of relics of the (often recent) past – things which might be called 'curiosities' rather than objects of archaeological interest. An antiquary was very often a minister of the Church, a doctor, schoolmaster or lawyer who enjoyed collecting as a hobby.
  Lawyer George Constable of Wallace-Craigie near Dundee was very probably the antiquary on whom Sir Walter *Scott* based the character of Jonathan Oldbuck of Monkbarns in the third of his *Waverley* novels, *The Antiquary*, published in 1816.
  A novel of manners whose action takes place in the last ten years of the eighteenth century, *The Antiquary* hinges on the circumstances of two

well-to-do Scottish families and their fisher neighbours.

The manuscript of *The Antiquary* is preserved in the Pierpont Morgan Library, New York. It is in this book that one of the most famous literary 'howlers' is to be found: in Chapter 7 Scott makes the sun *set* in the sea off the east coast of Scotland.

Apocryphal Tales Stories of doubtful authority, fictitious stories.

Many apocryphal tales are told about what people do when they have had 'one too many'. One such story is told of a customer in Edinburgh's *Sandy Bell's Bar* who was a native of Galloway. One of his favourite songs was the traditional 'Bonnie Gallowa'':

Oh, the Gallowa' hills are covered wi' broom,
Wi' heather bells and bonnie doons.
Wi' heather bells and rivers a'
And I'll gang oot ower the hills tae Gallowa'.

doons – downs; *gang* – go; *ower* – over

One evening in the pub the Galloway man got into conversation with an American who was touring Scotland. He extolled the beauties of Scotland and, most of all, Galloway. And, of course, he sung the stranger 'Bonnie Gallowa'', telling him how he longed to go 'hame tae Gallowa'. As the evening wore on the Scotsman became more and more maudlin, eventually falling asleep muttering 'tak' me hame tae Gallowa'.' The stranger, feeling sorry for him, took him at his word and bundled him into his car to set off for the district of Galloway, over 100 kilometres south-west of Edinburgh. After a couple of hours driving, the American woke his passenger with the words, 'We're in Galloway now. You'll have to direct me to your home,' whereupon the Scotsman told him to turn the car round and drop him off back at the pub, since he had lived almost next door to it for the last twenty years.

At least, that is the story he told his wife when he

arrived home, rather the worse for wear, at 4.00 a.m.

Appin Murder In 1752, forty-four-year-old Colin Campbell of Glenure, the Crown factor (estate manager), was murdered. Though a certain James of the Glen was hanged for the crime, to this day no one knows who really shot the man known as the 'Red Fox'.

The people of Edinburgh expressed great concern about the organization and conduct of the trial at the time. Held at Inverary, the stonghold of the Campbell *clan,* with the jury full of Campbells out for revenge, the trial was certainly not a fair one. After the hanging, the removal of James's bones from the gibbet at Ballachulish to be wired and hung above the ferry brought much protest. The Campbells insisted, however, saying that the sight of the skeleton hanging there for years would serve as a warning to others not to cross clan Campbell.

Over the centuries several different candidates have been proposed as the murderer, including Allan Oig, the son of James of the Glen. One theory in local folklore is that the Stewarts of Ballachulish organized a shooting match where the first prize was to be the privilege of shooting the factor. The match was won by Donald Stewart who duly shot Campbell. Other people around Appin believe that a man called Alan Breck Stewart was the murderer. In his novel *Kidnapped* (1886), *Stevenson* makes him an accomplice in the murder. Until at least the beginning of the twentieth century the Stewarts claimed to have known the true identity of the killer whose name was handed down under a vow of silence to certain members of the family.

April Fool's Day People who play tricks on each other on 1 April are probably celebrating a Celtic spring festival. The new year started on 25 March in the Celtic calendar so 1 April, coming seven days later, was the last day before the New Year festivities ended and life returned to normal.

3

In Scotland April Fool's Day tricks are called 'hunting the gowk' (cuckoo) or 'huntygowk' and the person caught out is called a 'gowk'. The tricks must be played before 12 noon so if someone tries to play a trick after this time they are told:

Huntygowk's past and you're a fool at last.

Armstrong, Johnny 'Gude night and joy be wi' you a'.'

> O, this is my departing time,
> For here nae langer maun I stay;
> There's not a friend or foe o' mine
> But wishes that I were away.
> What I hae done, for lack o' wit,
> I never, never can reca';
> I trust ye're a' my friends as yet,
> Gude night and joy be wi' you a'.

maun – must; *reca'* – recall; *a'* – all

This was the usual parting song in Scotland before the custom of singing '*Auld Lang Syne*' ousted it in the early nineteenth century. The words were supposedly written by the Border highwayman and freebooter Johnny Armstrong just before he was executed, in June 1660, for his part in the murder of Sir John Carmichael of Edrom, warden of the Marches in the Borders of Scotland.

Both words and tune are given in *The Border Minstrelsy* by Sir Walter *Scott*. The tune, which first appeared in Playford's *Scotch Tunes* in 1700 was used by *Burns* for his song 'The Farewell' written for the brethren of St James's Lodge, Tarbolton.

Arthur's Seat A large, lion-shaped hill in Edinburgh. The name has nothing to do with the legendary King Arthur, but is a corruption of the Gaelic *Ard-na-said* – 'the height of the arrows', and so may have been a place where people went to practise shooting.

Five local boys found more than they bargained for when they went hunting rabbits on Arthur's

4

Seat one day in 1836 for they stumbled into a hole containing seventeen tiny coffins. Each one was only four inches long and had a lid fixed on with brass pins. The boys gave the coffins to their teacher who removed the lids, revealing tiny, perfectly carved wooden figures. Many people believed at the time that the coffins were made by a *witch*, but no one came forward to claim them. Some of the coffins can be seen today in the Royal Museum of Scotland in Edinburgh.

Atholl Brose

> Charm'd with a drink which Highlanders compose,
> A German traveller exclaim'd with glee,
> Potztausend! sare, if dis is Athol Brose,
> How goot dere Athol Boetry must be!
>
> Thomas Hood

This drink, concocted for his soldiers by the Duke of Atholl, supposedly makes people strong.

For a single portion mix together ¼ pint (150 ml) whipped double cream with 2 tablespoons (30 ml) of clear honey and 3 tablespoons (45 ml) of whisky. Add 1 ounce (25 g) of toasted oatmeal and some blaeberries and raspberries to this mixture. Some people like to add 1 tablespoon (15 ml) of lemon juice.

AT Index Many of the folk-tales told in Scotland have their parallels in tales from other countries. The Finnish scholar Antii Aarne started to list and classify all of the tales of the world in a catalogue which he called *The Types of the Folk-tale*. As with the *Child Ballads*, every type of story is classified and given a number – *The Twa Humpy-Backit Laddies* (see *Fairy*) for example, is a version of AT 503 'The Gifts of the Little People'. The work was expanded by Stith Thompson of the University of Indiana. It is known as the Aarne-Thompson Index or AT Index for short.

Auld Alliance The Scots name for the centuries-old relationship between Scotland and France, often in alliance against the *Auld Enemy*, England.

Some stories tell that the long-standing friendship between the two countries started as early as the eighth century when the country of Scotland was still divided amongst the *Picts* and the Scots. Though they fought with each other, the Picts and Scots often banded together to fight against their common enemy the Saxons – the forefathers of the English.

The Saxons were a warlike people and even Emperor Charlemagne, the greatest ruler in Europe at that time, dreaded them. None the less, together the Picts and Scots appeared to be a match for the Saxons, for though they had gained a foothold south of the Forth they were unable to push further into Scotland. The story goes that Charlemagne sent envoys to the Scottish court offering to invade England if the Saxons should threaten Scotland, on the understanding that the Scots should reciprocate if the Saxons invaded France. The Scots agreed and the bond was firmly fixed when a company of Scots knights went to France to form the first troop of French Scots Guards.

To show that Scotland was allied to France the Scots standard showing a red *lion* rampant (standing on its hind legs) was surrounded with a double row of fleurs-de-lis, the emblem of France.

Another story tells that the Auld Alliance was formed in the fifteenth century when the Scots joined the war on the side of the French not long after the Battle of Agincourt. They fought their first battle on French soil against the English Duke of Clarence and his army at the village of Baugé, in the Anjou region. Clarence was killed and the Scots were victorious. The king of France made the leader of the Scots army High Constable, one of the highest titles in France and rewarded many of the Scottish nobles with French lands and châteaux to cement the alliance. Even today, a very fine Bordeaux comes from a vineyard with a Scottish name – Château Montrose.

Auld Enemy England is traditionally the 'old enemy' of Scotland as the Scots have felt themselves

6

under threat from English domination for centuries.
(See *Auld Alliance*.)

Auld Hornie The 'old horned-one', the *Devil*, so-called because of his horns.

The worship of a horned god Cernunnos (Celtic *cerne* – horn) was prevalent in Celtic society before the Roman invasion of Britain in 54BC.

Auld Kirk, the A name given to two very different well-known things – the Church of Scotland and *whisky*.

Auld Lang Syne

> Should auld acquaintance be forgot,
> And never brought to mind?
> Should auld acquaintance be forgot,
> And auld lang syne?
>
> For auld lang syne, my dear,
> For auld lang syne,
> We'll tak' a cup o' kindness yet,
> For auld lang syne.
>
> And there's a hand my trusty fiere!
> And gi'es a hand o' thine!
> And we'll tak' a richt gude-willie
>   waught,
> For auld lang syne.

lang syne – long ago; *tak'* – take; *fiere* – friend; *a richt gude-willie waught* – drink with good will

This old song, which has been traced in *broadsides* published prior to the close of the seventeenth century, was polished up by Robert *Burns*, in 1788. It is probably the most famous song in the world, being used at the end of parties and dances and to close political rallies.

Nowadays only the first verse, chorus and last verse are sung as a closing song (as above).

7

Everyone stands in a circle holding hands and sings verse one and the chorus. Many people want to start with the arms crossed but this is wrong. Only when the last verse starts, with the words 'And there's a hand my trusty fiere' are the hands released, the arms crossed and hands re-clasped. The arms are then shaken up and down as if shaking hands. Still with crossed arms the chorus is sung again and this time everyone walks or trots into the middle of the floor and back again.

Auld Mahoun Another name for the *Devil*, probably derived from Mohammed who was imagined to be a pagan god in the Middle Ages.

Auld Reekie This is the pet name for Edinburgh Old (*Auld*) Town because it used to be covered in a pall of smoke (*reek*).

Ayrshire Poet A name for Robert *Burns* (1759–96) who was born in Alloway in Ayrshire.

B

Bagpipe The history of the bagpipe is obscure. Related to instruments in which a whole reed is taken into the mouth, it was known as early as Roman times. An air reservoir in the form of a bag is inflated by air from the mouth and by a bellows movement of the player's arms. Because the reeds are sounded from the bag and not from the mouth directly, the player can breathe while playing and produce an uninterrupted sound. Bagpipes are found in Asia, North Africa and Europe.

The Scottish bagpipe comprises a *tartan* bag with a conical chanter, or melody pipe, and three drones (bass pipes) inserted into it. The drones provide the humming sound which can be heard under the melody as a monotonous tone. Bagpipes figure in Scottish regimental bands and in folk-music.

The *MacCrimmons*, the legendary pipers of

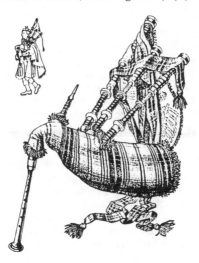

Skye, were said to have received the art of piping by some supernatural means.

Baliol, John Elected King of Scots in 1292, two years after the death of the *Maid of Norway*. John Baliol was given the nickname 'Toom Tabard' (empty coat); even though he looked rather fine in his rich robes, he was a weakling.
(See *Bruce, Heart of Bruce*.)

Ballads Traditional solo story-telling songs with the same music repeated for each verse. Covering a very wide range of subjects, including the death or dishonour of a high-ranking person, a supernatural theme, or the history of a battle, the Scottish ballads have been given the name 'The Muckle Sangs' (the big songs) and are considered the aristocrats of Scottish *folk-music*.
(See *Bothy Ballads, Broadside Ballads, Child Ballads, Scott*.)

Banshee In Scotland this means simply a *fairy* woman. The word comes from Scots Gaelic, *Ban* – woman and *sith* (adjective) – spiritual. The English use of the word to mean a spirit which appears and howls when someone is going to die, comes from Irish Gaelic.

Baptism Nowadays the Church of Scotland baptizes children from the age of about six weeks, though it used to be widely believed that a child should be baptized as soon as possible after birth in case it was taken away by the *fairy* folk. It could be protected until its baptism by putting a piece of *iron* in the cradle. In some places it was considered unlucky to call a child by its name before baptism.
(See *Birth*.)

Bard A Celtic poet and singer who wandered from place to place telling stories and reciting verses which he had often composed himself.
In the nineteenth century the name for the town of Balephuil in Tiree was 'Baile nam Bárd' ('the township of the bards') because many men and women were known as talented bards there. Their

songs and stories tell us about the traditions and history of the island and the people of Tiree; in particular about the families who emigrated to Canada in the nineteenth century. Many also tell of feats of strength and the daring life of the local hero, 'Strong' Archibald Maclean.

One such story, recorded by Margaret Mackay of the *School of Scottish Studies* and printed in the School's magazine *Tocher* (number 32), tells of how the custom of hanging the last man to pay his rent on the island was stopped by 'Strong' Archibald.

One rent day 'Strong' Archibald went to the Island House to pay his dues and arrived just slightly ahead of his neighbour, Donald MacKinnon. Donald was worried when he arrived, for everyone knew about the tradition of hanging the last man to pay his rent so he was quite surprised when 'Strong' Archibald told him to go in first. Now the factor (estate manager) had seen the two men walking across the field and he was also surprised to see Donald MacKinnon come in before 'Strong' Archibald. None the less, he took the rent from Donald and waited for the other man to come. When 'Strong' Archibald finally came in the factor said, 'You're the last to pay the rent this time. You know what that means?'

'Of course,' replied 'Strong' Archibald.

'Why didn't you come in before MacKinnon when you got here first?' asked the factor.

'I had some business to attend to,' was the reply.

'Well, you know what's going to happen to you, since you're the last,' said the factor.

'I do,' said 'Strong' Archibald. But as he said this he jumped up and grabbed the factor by the throat saying, 'But you'll die before me!'

The factor begged for mercy but 'Strong' Archibald would only let him go if he promised that there would be no more hangings, which he did. To make sure, 'Strong' Archibald threatened to come back and strangle the factor good and proper if there were – even if that meant that he should hang himself. And that put an end to the hangings in Tiree.

Bees A beehive is considered to be closely linked with the owners of the hive, and so when someone in the family dies it is important to tell the bees. If they are not told of the *death* they will fly away somewhere else.

Beltane This is the name for May Day in Scotland. The name and the celebrations connected with it go back to an ancient Celtic festival in which *bonfires* were lit on hill tops. Cattle were driven between the flames of these fires to protect them from disease.

Many young women believe that to wash their faces in the first dew of May will make them beautiful and in Edinburgh they climb to the top of *Arthur's Seat* to do this. There is also a religious service at the top of the hill on the same day.

Bible In many parts of Scotland the Bible is used as a means of *fortune telling*. Some Scots open the Bible at random on New Year's Day and place a finger on a passage without looking. The passage will foretell the reader's fortune in the coming year. Anyone wishing to find the answer to a troublesome problem can open the Bible at random and place their finger on any text. Whatever is written there is supposed to be of help.

Birds Birds are very often associated with bad *luck* in Scotland. If a caged bird dies on a wedding day, the marriage will be unhappy and the couple will separate soon. A bird flying into a room through an open window is an omen of death in the house.

The number of magpies seen in a field can predict the future. There are several versions of a rhyme which is said when magpies are about, the first one, from Lowland Scotland, contradicts the second, from Forfar in Angus:

> One for sorrow, two for joy,
> Three for a girl and four for a boy.
>
> Ane's joy, twa's grief,
> Three's a wedding, four's death.

An olds Scots belief was that the raven, normally thought of as a bird of ill-omen, provides the key to the secret of invisibility – a magic crystal. This is obtained by boiling the raven's eggs and returning them to the nest. The adult birds, knowing that something has happened to their eggs, leave the nest but, after three days, the male bird returns with a small piece of crystal in its beak. Anyone who possesses this crystal has the power of invisibility, achieved by putting the stone in his mouth.

Birth In times past it was common to unlock doors and to untie any knots on the clothing that the mother was wearing to ensure an easy birth. In recent years with almost all births taking place in hospital many of the old *superstitions* to do with birth have died out, but it is still believed that a child born with a caul over its head will never drown.
(See *Baptism*.)

Black Dwarfs These are good and helpful spirits who are known in every country where coal or minerals are mined. The Black Dwarfs live in the mines where they can sometimes be heard hammering and some people believe that if a miner follows the sound of their hammering he will find a vast amount of treasure. To thank the Dwarfs, it is usual to place some food at the entrance to the mine. Though Black Dwarfs are generally beneficent to miners they have been known to cause underground falls in order to stop miners whistling – a noise that they cannot tolerate.

Black Parliament At the beginning of the fourteenth century Edward I, the *'Hammer of the Scots'*, decided to try to get rid of William *Wallace* who was proving to be such a good leader in the Scottish War of Independence. Edward invited Wallace and the other Scots nobles to a council meeting near the town of Ayr. Suspecting no evil, the nobles arrived in twos and threes at the place where the meeting was to be held, the Barns of Ayr, a big wooden house just outside the town. Everything seemed quiet and peaceful, but as each man entered the barn he was seized, a rope was put round his neck and he was hanged from the beams of the roof. One after the other, the Scots nobles entered the barn, never to come out again.

A woman who was suspicious crept up to the barn and, seeing what was going on, intercepted Wallace on his way to Ayr. That night, as the English soldiers slept, the same woman went through the town putting a mark on every house which had an English soldier in it. Wallace and his men came after her, setting fire to the houses. Since all of the houses were made of wood, the whole place went up in flames in no time. Anyone who managed to escape the flames was quickly killed by Scots swords so that all that remained in the morning were dead bodies among the smoking ruins.

(See *Friar of Ayr's Blessing.*)

Bloody Butcher, the The Duke of Cumberland (1721–65), second son of George II, so called because he gave no quarter to the wounded and fleeing Scots soldiers after the Battle of *Culloden*.

Royalist publications of the time reported that after the battle the duke walked over the field in deep thought and was heard to say, 'Lord, what am I that I should be spared, when so many brave men lie dead upon the spot.' An authenticated story presents another side of the coin, however. Riding over the field to survey the bodies, the duke saw a young wounded Highlander who was resting on his elbow and staring at the royal party. He asked the man who he belonged to and was given the answer, 'the prince'. The duke commanded an officer to 'shoot that insolent scoundrel', but the officer, Major Wolfe, refused, saying that he was a soldier and not an executioner. The duke asked several other officers to perform the task, but since all refused the duty was given to a common soldier who happened to be nearby. The Highlander who was killed was Charles Fraser of Inverallachy, lieutenant-colonel of the Master of Lovat's regiment.

Blue Blanket Many stories concern the origin of this standard. Some people believe it was the flag of an ancient Roman Catholic order created by Pope Urban II in the thirteenth century. Others say it accompanied Edinburgh knights to the Crusades. It was, in fact, embroidered by Queen Margaret in 1482 and given to the craftsmen of Edinburgh by James III in gratitude to them for having freed him from prison in 1481.

Over the centuries the flag became a rallying point for the people in time of war and even today, every citizen of Scotland is supposed to rally round the Blue Blanket if their sovereign needs help.

Blue Bonnets An old term for the Scots. Up until the beginning of the twentieth century Scotsmen wore a flat bonnet made of dark blue cloth. The bonnet was later given the name 'Tammy' in honour of *Burns's* Tam o' Shanter who wore such a bonnet.

Bonfire (From 'bone-fire' – a fire made out of bones.) The lighting of bonfires on certain days in Scotland probably goes back to the old Celtic religion, where the hearth was the sacred centre of the house.

The power to make fire was what distinguished man from the animals and fire itself was sacred. Not only did it provide warmth and light, especially needed in northern countries, but it also protected against evil.

However, kindling a fire was a laborious procedure so household fires were usually kept going and carried from one place to another. On certain holy days all the household fires were extinguished and new fires were made. The fire-worshippers did this by rubbing a stick in an oak log, strengthening the new fire by dancing round it sunwise. Household fires were re-lit and kept going until the following fire festival. Days on which new fires were traditionally lit were *Hogmanay*, *Beltane*, Midsummer's Day and *Hallowe'en*.

Bonnie Dundee

To the Lords of Convention 'twas
    Claver'se who spoke,
'Ere the king's crown shall fall there are crowns
    to be broke;
Then each cavalier who loves honour and me,
Let him follow the bonnet of Bonnie Dundee.

Sir Walter Scott

Depending on whether you were a *Whig* or a *Jacobite*, John Graham of Claverhouse, Viscount of Dundee, was either a follower of the *Devil* or a great hero and genius of command whose death at the Battle of Killiecrankie in 1689 left his troops in disarray.

Called 'Bloody Claverse' by those loyal to the royalist cause, he had, according to them, sold his soul to the Devil. Stories were told of how he could turn wine to clotted blood and could boil cold water by touching it with his foot. The royalist version of his death was that he was killed by a silver button fired by his own servant.

The Highlanders, on the other hand, referred to him as 'Bonnie Dundee' and rallied to his call to battle on behalf of the *Old Pretender* at the narrow pass of Killiecrankie. Though facing more than twice as many regular soldiers, Dundee's army fought well and bravely, charging through the royal troops and forcing them to retreat. The victory was lost, however, with the death of Dundee, without whose command the Highland men could not be kept together.

Bonnie Moorhen

My bonnie moorhen has feathers ae new,
They are all fine colours but nane o' them's blue,
She's red and she's white and she's green
    and she's grey,
My bonnie moorhen, come hither away.
ae – ever; *nane* – none

Songs written by the sympathizers of *Bonnie Prince Charlie* were forbidden for a long time after the rebellion of 1745. Nothing daunted, Jacobite songwriters developed a number of codes to refer to their prince. Written to describe the prince's wanderings after the Battle of *Culloden* the song 'My Bonnie Moorhen' uses the metaphor of the moorhen to describe the prince in exile. The colours in the bird's feathers are found in the Stuart *tartan*.

Bonnie Prince Charlie

> Charlie is my darling,
> My darling, my darling,
> Oh, Charlie is my darling,
> The young Chevalier.

Charles Edward Louis Casimir Stuart (1720–88), also called the 'Young Chevalier' or the 'Young Pretender' (i.e., claimant to the English throne), was the son of James Stuart, the *Old Pretender*, and great-grandson of James VI. A look at the following family tree will help to clarify the relationships in the Stuart family.

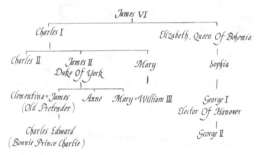

When Charles's grandfather, James II, tried to impose his Roman Catholicism on the people he was deposed. The throne was given to William and Mary, nephew and daughter of James, passed on to James's second daughter Anne and, after her death, by Act of Parliament to the nearest Protestant heir, George, Elector of Hanover.

George I was scarcely on the throne when friends of James Stuart, calling themselves the *Jacobites*, raised an insurrection in 1715. This rebellion was suppressed and George had a relatively peaceful reign until his death in 1727. Meanwhile, James Stuart married Clementina, granddaughter of John Sobieski, the heroic king of Poland and had two sons, one of whom was Charles Edward, known in Scotland as 'Bonnie Prince Charlie'.

Like many real and famous people, the name of Bonnie Prince Charlie has had so much folklore attached to it that it has become difficult to disentangle historical fact from fiction. For some people he is a hero who should rightfully have been king of Scotland, while others believe he was a drunk, a fop and a liar who wasted the flower of Scottish manhood in his attempts to get himself the throne of Scotland. Charles's letters show him to have been not particularly bright, and he enjoyed hunting and sport much more than book learning. Like his father, he believed in the divine right of kings and, perhaps for this reason, along with his love of action, he allowed himself to be manipulated by the Church and state who used him as the figurehead in their attempts to gain control of the crown in the rebellion of 1745 – 1746. Charles and his supporters were defeated at *Culloden* in 1746 and Charles, after wandering in the Highlands for some time with a price of £30000 on his head, escaped to France. The bonnie prince never returned to Scotland but remained in exile on the continent, living a dissipated life until his death in Rome in 1788.

(See also *Bonnie Moorhen; Fifteen; Forty-five; Macdonald; Seven Men of Glenmoriston; Seven Men of Moidart; Prince's Strand.*)

Bothy Ballads

> The ploughman he's a bonnie lad,
> And does his wark at leisure,
> And when that he comes hame at e'en,
> He kisses me wi' pleasure.

Bothy ballads are folk-songs dealing with the everyday lives of the itinerant farmworkers of north-east Scotland in the nineteenth century. The songs deal with love, courtship, marriage, domestic life, farm life and work and also include patriotic songs and *ballads*.

One of the best collections of bothy ballads was made at the beginning of the twentieth century by Superintendent John Ord of the Glasgow Police Force. Many of the songs in Ord's collection are still sung today by traditional and not so traditional folk-singers. Ord notes in his collection that the old version of 'The Ploughman' was preferred not only in the north-east, but throughout the whole of Scotland.

Brahan Seer Kenneth the Sallow or Coinneach Odhar, a man who possessed the gift of *second sight,* worked as a labourer on the Brahan Estate, Maryburgh, near Dingwall. Though he was born more than 300 years ago, the prophesies which he made and the things which he foretold are still discussed in Scotland.

About 150 years before the construction of the Caledonian Canal, the Brahan Seer prophesied the linking of the chain of lochs from the Moray Firth to Loch Linnhe. Telford's 100-kilometre-long stretch of water, connecting the North Sea with the Atlantic, was opened in 1822. At a time and place where there were virtually no roads, the Seer prophesied that 'the day will come when there will be a road through the hills of Ross, and a bridge upon every stream.' Sceptics say that anyone could foretell such developments but the vision which he related at *Culloden* can only have appeared to someone with the sight. Standing on the place where one of the bloodiest battles in the history of Scotland was to be fought, the Brahan Seer was recorded as saying, 'This bleak moor, ere many generations have passed, shall be stained with the best blood of Scotland.'

Broadside Ballads Almost as soon as printing was invented ballads and songs began to be published on one side of a single sheet of cheap paper and sold for a few pennies at *fairs* or on the streets. These compositions were usually based on real events and were often gruesome, dealing with murders or hangings. Because the paper on which they were printed was broader than it was long, the songs became known as 'broadside ballads'.

Broonie Country people believe in this *fairy* who helps about the house. Small and brown, the broonie is happy to be paid with a bowl of porridge and cream. If a housewife, trying to be kind, gives the broonie a suit of clothes, he will leave her house for ever.

Sometimes the broonie comes to teach people a lesson or to test people. He disguises himself as a tramp and asks for food. If someone gives him food, thinking he is a tramp, that is a good person. Someone who turns a tramp away, refusing to help him, is bad.

Bruce, Robert the Elected king of Scotland from 1306 until his death in 1329, Robert the Bruce is best known for having defeated the English under Edward I, the '*Hammer of the Scots*', at Bannockburn in 1314. Bruce had, however, originally fought for Edward, joining him, not only because he was an English as well as a Scottish lord, but because he hated John *Baliol,* who had been made king in 1292.

Bruce probably hoped that by helping Edward defeat Baliol, he himself would be put on the throne. However, when Baliol gave up his right to the throne of Scotland and placed himself at Edward's mercy, Edward put English governors into the Scottish castles and rejected Bruce's plea to be made King of Scotland.

The best-known story about Robert the Bruce tells that when he was in hiding and thinking of giving up his fight against Edward, he lay on a bed in a cave and watched a spider. The spider tried many times to climb to the roof up its web, but just did not manage it. The spider tried and tried and eventually succeeded. Bruce was encouraged by this and he, too, decided to try again.

20

Burke and Hare William Burke and William Hare have gone down in Scottish folk history as two of the most evil men. In the early nineteenth century, when the science of anatomy was in its infancy, Burke and Hare, two Irishmen who came to Scotland to work as labourers on the construction of the Union Canal, provided bodies to surgeons working at Edinburgh's School of Anatomy.

Starting off by selling the body of a man who had died of natural causes, Burke and Hare quickly turned to murder to ensure a constant supply of bodies for their main customer, Dr Knox. Between February and October 1828, the two men lured sixteen unsuspecting victims into Hare's lodging house in the West Port, made them drunk on cheap whisky and then smothered them. At the beginning of their careers they were almost discovered when a medical student recognized the body of a young girl he knew, but, as Burke and Hare deliberately chose their victims from people who were on the edge of society – tramps, orphans, prostitutes and beggars – it was thought that the girl had probably died of drink. They were eventually caught when a visitor found the body of a woman in Hare's room.

The trial of Burke and Hare, which took place on Christmas Eve 1828, lasted only twenty-four hours. Hare turned king's evidence to escape punishment, but had to flee in secret to Ireland to avoid being lynched by the people of Edinburgh. Burke was taken first to Calton Jail then, on 28 January 1829, he was hanged before an estimated crowd of 20000. His only complaint was that Dr Knox had not paid for the last body. Needless to say, Knox himself disappeared from the medical scene after this and lived the rest of his life as a recluse.

Burns, Robert

> Robin was a rovin' boy,
> Rantin' rovin', rantin' rovin';
> Robin was a rovin' boy,
> Rantin' rovin' Robin.

Robert Burns was born in Alloway, Ayrshire on 25
January 1759. His parents were William Burnes
from Kincardineshire (1721–84), who ran a seven-
acre tenant farm in Alloway, and Agnes Broun of
Maybole (1732–1820). The family moved to
seventy-acre Mount Oliphant, near Alloway, in
1766 and later to Lochlie, Tarbolton, a 130-acre
farm. From an early age Burns and his brother
Gilbert helped their father, a God-fearing and
hard-working Calvinist. It was this hard farming
work, begun too early in life, which probably
contributed to the heart trouble which, acceler-
ated by rheumatism, was to lead to the poet's early
death.

On occasion Burns and some of his biographers
encouraged the belief that his poetry was a gift
from 'the Muses', a natural talent which sprung
from the innocence of country life. But, though he
worked at the plough from an early age, Burns was
in reality no 'natural genius', having first attended
Alloway Mill village school, which had been
established by his father and some other villagers
and later, Hugh Rodger's school, Kirkoswald.
When the family moved to Mount Oliphant,
Burns's education was continued by his father and
by his own study of literature, politics, theology
and philosophy. He also read Allan Ramsay and
Robert Fergusson, who had collected some of the
ancient Scots poems and written new ones based
on these ancient models.

Burns, like every eighteenth-century Scot, was
well-versed in the Bible and the metrical versions
of the Psalms, and heard a great deal of pulpit
oratory which drew heavily on these sources. His
early influences were not only religious, however,
for two long-standing Scottish traditions played a
major part in his education: the *oral tradition* of
folk-song and story and the highly developed
literary tradition which goes back as far as the
Middle Ages and the Scottish Chaucerians, Henry-
son, Dunbar and Douglas.

By the age of twenty-seven Burns had written all
but a few of his greatest long poems. Acclaimed
Caledonia's bard, he was invited to Edinburgh

where he arrived on 28 November 1786, riding on a borrowed pony with the remains of the £20 profits from the Kilmarnock edition of his poems in his pocket. During his stay in the capital, he came into contact with some of the best minds in Scotland and proved himself equal to them in conversation and debate. Well known for his fondness for women, it was in Edinburgh that Burns met his most famous love, *'Clarinda'* – Mrs Agnes McLehose.

In 1788 Burns was given a commission as an excise officer or tax inspector and he settled down at Ellisland, near Dumfries, married his long-standing love Jean Armour and combined his official duties with farming, family life and writing and collecting songs. This, Burns's fourth farm, failed like its predecessors, so he moved his family to Dumfries where they were fairly happy despite a chronic shortage of money and Burns's recurrent illnesses.

Burns's reputation as a womanizing reckless wastrel who burnt himself out through drink and excess has remained with him through the centuries since his death. True, his health was not good and he was given to bouts of depression and nervous exhaustion, but this was quite likely due to having had to work hard on the farm as an adolescent rather than dissipation. A look at the amount of work which Burns did during the last years of his life must also refute any claim that he was a waster.

From 1789 to 1791 he carried the burden of his losing bargain on the steep and stony ground of Ellisland farm as well as doing the full-time work of an excise officer. At the same time he edited *The Scots Musical Museum,* an anthology of Scottish folk-songs brought out by the engraver James Johnson, and also collected, restored and imitated many of the songs which appeared in several of the volumes. He also collected for George Thomson's *Select Collection of Original Scottish Airs* and, though badly in need of money, anonymously and voluntarily wrote words to many of the tunes which appeared therein. Burns wrote over

300 songs, including love songs and bawdry, as well as songs about drink, work, friendship and patriotism.

Burns Supper

> For a' that, and a' that,
> It's coming yet, for a' that,
> That man to man the warld o'er
> Shall brothers be for a' that.

On 25 January, Scots and non-Scots all over the world get together for an evening of eating, drinking and entertainment to celebrate the birth of Scotland's national poet, Robert *Burns*.

The evening starts with *Scottish country dancing* interspersed with songs and recitations of Burns's poems – almost always 'Tam o' Shanter' and the 'Address to the Unco Guid'. A meal is served, during which more poems are recited and speeches are made.

The meal should include *haggis,* accompanied by the traditional turnip and mashed potato. After a recitation of 'To a Haggis' the haggis is 'piped' in to the room (preceded by a piper playing a rousing tune) and ceremoniously cut with a sgian-dubh (pronounced 'ski-an doo'), the small knife that Scotsmen wearing a kilt have in the tops of their hose or stocking. *Whisky* is taken to drink various toasts, including one 'Tae the Lassies'. One of the lassies (women) replies to this with a toast to the men. After the meal the dancing begins and, like other gatherings, the Burns Supper ends with *'Auld Lang Syne'*.

Some Scots think that Burns Suppers are just an excuse for sentimentalizing and criticize the self-consciousness of many of the quasi-philosophers who speak at them. However, it should be remembered that, like *St Andrew's Night* get-togethers, Burns Suppers are well respected outside Scotland as being not only good meeting places for expatriot Scots, but also providing a link between Scots emigrants and their hosts. Burns's poems and songs have been translated into almost every different known language and people from vastly different cultures can quote Burns in the original. This international appeal stems in part from Burns's ability to portray the human condition, but more so from his democratic ideas of liberty, equality and fraternity and his love of common humanity.

C

Caledonia The Latin name for Scotland.
(See *Alba, Dalriada, Scotia.*)

Candlemas 2 February. One of the *quarter-days* in
Scotland. An old Scottish *weatherlore* saying
goes:

> If Candlemas Day be dry and fair,
> The half o' winter's come and mair.
> If Candlemas Day be wet and foul
> The half o' winter was gone at Yule.

mair – more

The word comes from the consecration of the
candles which will be needed in the Roman
Catholic Church for the following year.

Ceilidh (pronounced 'kay-lee') A party for people
of all ages where *sgeultachdan* (pronounced
'skèllt-achg-tan') are told and *ballads* are sung.
More often than not a ceilidh provides a good
excuse for a dance, though amongst older people
the sgeultachdan are the high point of the

evening. These are stories which have almost never been written down. They very often have a theme suited to the occasion on which they are told and sometimes contain a moral. A *sgeultair* (narrator) can be so skilful that the stories are told in rhyme.

Chambers, Robert (1802–71) The picture that is normally conjured up of an *antiquary* is that of an old, grey-haired man, stooped and covered in dust from his old books and papers. However, in March 1824, when Robert Chambers published the first part of a serial collection of folklore called *Traditions of Edinburgh* he was aged only twenty-two. A second volume was dedicated to Sir Walter Scott who had been so impressed by the early numbers of the volume that he had asked in all astonishment 'where the boy got all the information'.

Not long after the first volume of the *Traditions* was completed, Scott gave 'the boy' some material to use in further work. This consisted of sixteen close-written pages containing reminiscences of old Edinburgh people and things.

Scott continued to be generous and contributed to Chambers's next work, *The Popular Rhymes of Scotland* (published 1826) which was followed by *Scottish Jests and Anecdotes* (1832) including a section called 'Mots of Sir Walter Scott'.

By the age of thirty, Chambers had published three collections based on *oral tradition,* each one exploring different facets of the life of the people of Scotland.

Together with his brother William, Robert Chambers became a partner in a publishing firm and spent the next three decades of his life as an active publisher, editor and author. All of this work took him away from folklore, which he returned to only with his last work, *The Book of Days* (1862–4), a fascinating two-volume work containing various articles and illustrations for each day of the year, ranging from 'The Death and Funeral of a Squaw in London', and 'The Deaths of some Ancient Widows' to 'The Primitive style of

Skating'. He records the coldest day of the century as 20 January 1838 and reports on some 'Early notices of Coffee'.

Changeling A changeling replaces a real baby stolen by a *fairy*. Since it has been put into the cradle to get human milk, it is usually very hungry and cantankerous, crying and moaning all day long.

To get the real baby back it is necessary to throw the changeling into water or fire. In order to be sure that a crying child really is a changeling and not just a fractious baby, the changeling-baby is made to speak and show that it is an old man. One way of doing this is to make a ring of half eggshells filled with water. The changeling will then ask what the eggs are for. When it is then told that the ring is a brewing cauldron it usually replies that it has never seen such a thing in all its life. This is the clue that tells the mother that the being in the cradle is no child of hers. She can then throw it on the fire or in water and get her own child back.

Charm A spell or rhyme which wards off bad *luck*. Scottish children for example say the following protective charm when they see an ambulance:

Hold my collar, be a scholar, never be an invalid.

As they say the rhyme, they hold the collar of their school blazer, shirt or blouse. In some parts of Scotland they must keep holding it until they see a four-footed animal, though in Aberdeen, spitting on the ground is enough after saying the charm. In this way the children believe they will stay out of hospital.

(See *Luck, Superstition*.)

Chevalier Polite name for *Bonnie Prince Charlie* or the *Old Pretender*. In full, the title was Chevalier St George.

Child Ballads How long the tradition of ballad singing has gone on in the British Isles no one knows, but many of the Scottish ballad texts which we know today were taken down from living Scottish tradition in the late eighteenth and early nineteenth century by various scholars and collectors. However, in the early stages only a few portions of the ballad texts had been published and these with so many editorial changes and distortions that they scarcely resembled their originals.

The most comprehensive collection of *ballads* was compiled in the late nineteenth century by Harvard University professor Francis James Child (born Boston, 1 February 1825) in the five-volume study, *The English and Scottish Popular Ballads* (published 1883–98).

The collection is made up of 305 ballads, with their variations, some of which run to ten or more versions. There is also a preface to each ballad which includes a comprehensive discussion of the history and the conjectured date of composition. The folklore behind the ballad, its place in different cultural traditions and how its subject is related to folk-tales from other parts of the world are also included. Child gave each ballad a number which is used by folklorists and scholars in the same way as the *AT Index*. The American professor Bertrand Harris Bronson put the tunes to the Child ballads in a four-volume work *Traditional Tunes of the Child Ballads* in 1959.

Many of the Child ballads were still being sung by *travelling people* at the time of the founding of the *School of Scottish Studies*. Fieldworkers from the school collected the ballads on tape and encouraged the singers to perform them for non-travellers at the time of the folk-music revival. The ballads are a living tradition in Scotland, sung not only by travelling people but by other folk-singers, both professional and amateur.

Children's Street Games A lot of folklore and old traditions are to be found in children's street games which contain elements of ritual and religion as well as evidence of the foreign contacts which have influenced the whole of Scotland.

SCOTTISH FOLKLORE

Many of the 'nonsense' words used as counting-
out rituals to start games are simply corruptions of
foreign languages. An Edinburgh favourite is:

> Ixey, kixey, calmonella
> I spy Jonah fella.
> Jonah fella calmonella,
> I spy toosh.

These words bear close resemblance to the
Finnish words for 'one, two, three' and were
probably introduced to Scotland by seamen.

In chasing and catching games where players
run out of breath and need a pause, the Scots child
licks his thumbs, holds them out and says
'Barleys' – a relic from the days of chivalry, the
word comes from the French 'parler'.

One very rough game in which 'Barleys' is often
used is 'King o' the Castle', where players try to
push each other down from a tree or a wall or
some other place of security, chanting 'I'm the
king o' the castle, get down you dirty wee rascal',
as they do so. This game may spring from an old
political root, for *Chambers* tells us in his *Popular
Rhymes* that when Oliver Cromwell asked the
governor of Home Castle, Berwickshire, to sur-
render in 1650 he was greeted with a chant of:

> I, Willy Wastle stand on my castle,
> And a' the dogs o' your toon
> Will no' drive Willy Wastle doon.

Games in which one or more players stand in
the middle of a circle while the others dance
round them probably relate to the old Celtic
religion and sun-worship. A favourite with girls all
over Scotland is 'The Dusty Bluebells' in which the
children stand in a circle holding their joined
hands up high to make archways. Using a suitable
counting-out ritual, one girl is chosen to stand in
the middle of the circle. When the following song
begins, she runs in and out through the arches or
'Dusty Bluebells'.

> In and out the dusty bluebells,
> In and out the dusty bluebells,
> In and out the dusty bluebells,
> I am your master.

On the last note of the word 'master' the girl stands behind another player in the circle and pats her lightly on the shoulders, singing:

> Pitter, pitter, patter on your shoulders,
> Pitter, pitter, patter on your shoulders,
> Pitter, pitter, patter on your shoulders,
> I am your master.

These two girls then continue in and out, patting the shoulders of a third girl and so on until all the players are in a long line, running as fast as possible until someone shouts stop.

The Scottish game of peevers (English hopscotch) may also be a relic of solar worship. Pliny records boys playing a game of round hopscotch and several diagrams with numbers can still be seen on the ancient pavement of the Roman Forum. The early Christians adopted the general idea of the game and converted it to Christianity, changing the shape of the form into that of the basilica of the early church. The game was then meant to represent the progress of the soul from heaven to earth.

See *Charm*.

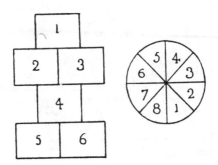

Clan (From the Gaelic *clann* – children, offspring, descendants.) *Chambers English Dictionary* defines a clan as 'a tribe or collection of families subject to a single chieftain, commonly bearing the same surname and supposed to have a common ancestor'.

The idea that the members of a tribe shared the same forefather was a myth which was commonly used to hold primitive societies together. The legendary circumstances of their birth and their heroic deeds were often told by the *bards*. In Scotland the *seannachie* or clan story-teller could always relate the genealogy of his particular clan. Tracing the ancestry back to very long ago, his story sometimes told that the first children born into the clan were the result of a union between the common ancestor and a supernatural being.

Clan surnames generally begin with the prefix 'Mac' or 'Mc', meaning 'son of', though every clan has septs (divisions) of people who do not have a name beginning with 'Mac'. Members of the septs can, nonetheless, wear the clan *tartan*.

Clarinda

> Ae fond kiss, and then we sever;
> Ae fareweel, and then for ever!
> Deep in heart-wrung tears I'll pledge thee,
> Warring sighs and groans I'll wage thee.

ae – one; *fareweel* – farewell

'Clarinda' was *Burns*'s name for Mrs Agnes McLehose, whom he met and fell in love with at the house of their mutual friend Mrs Nimmo in Edinburgh in December 1787.

No one has ever established the exact nature of their relationship, but letters that survive to 'Clarinda' from '*Sylvander*' (Burns) and some of Burns's letters to other friends suggest that they felt very passionately about each other. Burns, however, had to leave Clarinda to return to Ayrshire to settle some matters to do with Jean Armour.

Jean became his wife in April 1788 and the relationship between Burns and Clarinda cooled. Their final meeting was on 6 December 1791 when Mrs MacLehose recorded in her diary, 'This day I never can forget. Parted with Burns in the year 1791, never more to meet in this world. Oh, may we meet in heaven!' She died in 1831, aged eighty-two. Burns had died some thirty-five years before on 21 July 1796.

Perhaps one of the most beautiful songs Burns wrote is the love song 'Ae Fond Kiss' which describes his parting with Clarinda.

Claverhouse John Graham of Claverhouse, Viscount of Dundee.
(See *Bonnie Dundee*.)

Clootie A name for the *Devil*. It comes from the Scots word for a cloven hoof. People believe that though the Devil can change his shape, he can never get rid of his cloven hoofs.

Clootie was once known to have been engaged to marry a young woman who lived near Bennochie Hill in Aberdeenshire. Though Clootie had disguised himself as a handsome young man, the young woman discovered, on the day of the wedding, that her prospective bridegroom had cloven hoofs – a sure sign that he was the Devil. The young woman thought up all sorts of ideas in an attempt to put off the wedding but Clootie insisted that the wedding should go ahead. Finally she said she would marry him only if he would make a road from the foot to the top of Bennochie before she finished baking a quantity of bread. The Devil agreed and both started work but, just as she was baking the last loaf, Clootie reappeared and told her that the road was finished. He claimed her for his bride according to their bargain and carried her off by force. However, in passing Bennochie Hill she struggled so much that the Devil transformed her together with her girdle (iron baking plate) and spirtle (wooden spoon) into the three grey stones which, with the road he made on the hill, are pointed out to this day to show his wonderful power.

Coconut Tam In late nineteenth-century Edinburgh the small hunch-backed figure of Coconut Tam could be seen selling coconuts and calling out the street cry 'Cocky-nit, cocky-nit, a penny the bit!'

Columba Along with *St Andrew*, St Columba is the best known saint of Scotland. He is credited with bringing Christianity to Scotland. In AD563 Columba, together with twelve friends, sailed to Scotland from *Ireland* in a wickerwork boat. They landed on the island of Hy, renaming it 'Carn cul ri Erin' – 'The back turned upon Ireland' – and built a church there.

Columba and his priests converted many Scots to Christianity but the *Picts* were not so keen to be converted. The king of the Picts lived at Inverness so Columba set out to travel there. After a long and difficult journey Columba found the gates of the king's stronghold barred against him. Nothing daunted, Columba raised his hand and made the sign of the cross on the doors, which immediately flew open. When the king of the Picts heard about this he invited Columba in, heard his message of peace and was thus converted to Christianity.

St Columba's emblem is a bear.

Common Ridings During the summer months the Scottish Border towns hold various festivals called the Common Ridings. These are annual ceremonies in which each town lays claim to the ownership of common land which has been granted to it at some time in the past. Though varying in small details, all of the Common Ridings are similar.

In **Lauder**, bandsmen and cheering people watch the town's horsemen set off to ride around the boundaries of the town. The riders gather at one point to drink a glass of whisky with the Provost and the town band, after which they ride off to cover the rest of the extensive boundaries before returning to the town to be greeted again by the Provost with another drink in the town hall.

In **Selkirk** the celebrations are on the theme of

34

the Battle of *Flodden* (1513). Selkirk starts to prepare for the celebrations in May when a young man is chosen to be the town's standard bearer. This man must be Selkirk-born, single and have regularly taken part in previous Ridings. When he is elected, the town has a concert where traditional songs are sung. A speech is given telling of the town's history and particularly of how the news of the defeat of the Scots at Flodden was brought to Selkirk.

It is in June that the actual Selkirk Common Riding takes place. In the evening before the day of the Common Riding, known as 'the nicht afore the morn' – a town official announces that the next day will see the Riding of the Boundaries. This is called 'crying the burley'. There are parties and late night drinking. Next day the town is invaded by people who come from all over the world for the Riding.

Starting at 7.00 a.m. as many as 200 horses clatter through the town and out over the fields. A replica of the standard which was brought back from Flodden is carried in front followed by the town flag carried by the town's standard bearer. The riders cover about fourteen miles, riding as far as the Three Brethren, a mountain which lies between the Yarrow and the Tweed.

Returning into the town at about 9.00 a.m., a very solemn ceremony takes place. The two standards are 'cast' (laid down), to be followed by all the flags of the various guilds. New wreaths are placed on the Flodden memorial. The rest of the day is a holiday with much celebration.

In **Jedburgh**, the game of hand-ba' is played in the streets. It is said that the ball is the symbol of the head of the commander of the English garrison of Ferniehirst Castle.

The town of **Hawick** has the custom of beating small boys at its boundaries.

The other Border towns of Peebles, Galashiels, Melrose, Kelso, Innerleithen, Walkerburn, Stow, Earlston, Duns and Langholm also have Common Ridings, but their traditions were broken some time ago and what they do now is either reinvented tradition or only a small part of what was done before.

Due to fortuitous planning, all of the towns have their Common Ridings on different days, so it is quite possible to travel round the Borders, moving from one town to the next all through the summer.

Cope, Sir John

> General Cope led frae behind,
> Tae keep his men in order.
> When the English ran he was in the van,
> And first across the border.

frae – from

Cope was the commander of the English troops who fought against *Bonnie Prince Charlie* at Prestonpans, just south of Edinburgh on 20 September 1745. The Scots attacked before the English were awake and managed to rout them. Cope ran away and carried the news of his own defeat to Berwick.

Covenanters Scottish Presbyterians who signed various bonds or covenants pledging to advance Presbyterianism.

The earliest Covenant was entered into by the Lords of the Congregation in 1557 and another was authorized by James VI in 1581. It was in the early seventeenth century, however, that the Covenant became an issue for all classes of people when Charles I tried to impose Archbishop Laud's prayerbook on the Church. This act led to lots of ordinary people signing the Covenant in Edinburgh's Greyfriars Kirkyard in 1638. In 1643 the Covenanters pledged not only to preserve Presbyterianism in Scotland but also to help establish it along with their allies in England and Ireland. Though Covenants were outlawed in 1662, many Scots remained loyal to the Covenant and Presbyterianism, holding their religious services in the hills.

Culloden – 'They have devoured Jacob' The Battle of Culloden on 16 April 1746 was the turning point in the war of the *Jacobite* cause. The supporters of *Bonnie Prince Charlie*, ill-equipped, tired and hungry, faced nearly 9000 trained redcoats armed with muskets and cannon. Numbering approximately 4500, the Jacobite army included old men, deserters from foreign armies and unarmed children and the result was, predictably, annihilation for the Scots.

After the battle, instead of treating the wounded with humanity, the English soldiers under the *'Bloody Butcher'* Cumberland were ordered to kill any survivors lying wounded on the field. One soldier reported at the time that this killing was done more in sport than in rage and that because the English soldiers began splashing each other with blood they looked 'more like so many butchers than an army of Christian soldiers'.

After the slaughter it was the duty of the chaplain to read the service of the day. The service for the 16 April should commence with Psalm 79 which includes the words '. . . The dead bodies of thy servants have they given to be meat unto the fowls of heaven . . . Their blood have they shed like water . . . and there was none to bury them . . . they have devoured Jacob, and laid waste his dwelling place . . .' but according to tradition, an order to substitute another psalm was immediately given.

D

Dalriada The name for an ancient Scots/Irish kingdom with its central government in the region of Argyll.

Some time around the turn of the sixth century the region was divided amongst the three sons of the Irish king, Earc. Loarn took north Argyll, Angus looked after Islay and Fergus, who is supposed to have brought the *Stone of Destiny* to Scotland with him, administered Kintyre, Knapdale, Cowal and Mid-Lorn.

(See *Alba, Caledonia, Scotia.*)

Dandelion The dandelion is used as a clock by children in Scotland. They take the flower head when it has gone to seed and blow away the seeds, counting the number of puffs needed to get all the seeds away. That then is the time. These seed bits are also caught by children who call them wishes. Each seed head caught grants a wish but you must never tell anyone else what you have wished, otherwise your wish will not be granted.

Because of its diuretic properties, the dandelion has been given the folk-name 'piss-a-bed'. In France it has the same name, *'pissenlit'*.

Dawson, Jemmy

> The dismal scene was o'er and past,
> The lover's mournful hearse retired;
> The maid drew back her languid head,
> And sighing forth his name expir'd.
>
> Shenstone

James Dawson, a young Lancashire man who was a student at St John's College, Cambridge, joined *Bonnie Prince Charlie* in his fight against the

English at Carlisle. Dawson was hanged and quartered on Kennington Common in London, together with eight other rebels, on 30 July 1746, the date on which he should have married. Outwardly composed, his fiancée attended the execution accompanied by a man and one female friend. She watched everything, managing to restrain her emotions until the very end when she cried out, 'My dear, I follow thee, I follow thee – sweet Jesus, receive both our souls together!' and died.

Death A great number of *superstitions* are connected with death in Scotland. Many Scots people believe that a person will die more easily if all the doors and locks in the house are opened. In times past, a dying person was often lifted out of bed and laid on the floor to die so that his soul could return unhindered to the earth from which it came. In many Scots households, even today, people will not put a pair of shoes on the table for fear of provoking a death in the family. This superstition probably relates to the custom of passing on the dead person's wearable shoes and clothes to another member of the family.

(See *Birth, Funerals.*)

Declaration of Arbroath

> We have been set free by our most tireless Prince, King and Lord, the Lord Robert. Yet, if he should give up what he has begun, and agree to make us or our kingdom subject to the King of England or the English, we should exert ourselves at once to drive him out as our enemy and a subverter of his own rights and ours, and make some other man who was well able to defend us our King; for, as long as but a hundred of us remain alive, never will we on any conditions be brought under English rule. It is in truth not for glory, nor riches, nor honours that we are fighting, but for freedom – for that alone, which no honest man gives up but with life itself.

The Scottish Church played a critical part in the Wars of Independence, fought against the English from 1296 to 1328. Not only did the churchmen rally the lairds and barons to resist the English claims by preaching and fighting, but they also took the cause of Scotland to the court of Rome. The declaration of independence known as the Declaration of Arbroath was probably drawn up by Bernard of Linton, Abbot of Arbroath and Chancellor of Scotland. Written in polished Latin, it urges Pope John XXII to acknowledge the independence of the Scots to recognize Robert the *Bruce*, elected to the throne in 1306, as Scotland's rightful king. Signed on 6 April 1320 by Bruce and endorsed, signed and sealed by thirty-eight Scots lords, it also states that if Bruce should ever interfere with the freedom of the people of Scotland, he would be dethroned and replaced by another who would uphold their will and wishes.

(See the *Friar of Ayr's Blessing*.)

Derwentwater's Lights An Aberdeenshire name for the aurora borealis. James, Earl of Derwentwater, was beheaded on 24 February 1716, for supporting the *Old Pretender*. It is said that the aurora borealis was very bright on that night.

Scots people also call the aurora borealis the 'Merry Dancers'.

Devil

> O Thou, whatever title suit thee!
> Auld Hornie, Satan, Nick, or Clootie,
> Wha in yon cavern grim an' sooty
>   Clos'd under hatches,
> Spairges about the brunstane cootie,
>   To scaud poor wretches!
>
> *spairges* – spatters;   *brunstane* – brimstone;
> *scaud* – scauld

Burns

Though *Burns* calls the Devil 'Satan' in his 'Address to the De'il', the angel who challenged God should not be confused with the Devil whom the Scots know – a supernatural being more closely connected with the pagan goat god, Pan and often depicted with cloven hoofs. It is from these hoofs that the Devil gets one of his many nicknames, *'Clootie'*. No other character in Scots folklore has as many names as the Devil, among them, *'Auld Hornie'*, 'Auld Nick', *'Auld Mahoun'* and the 'Earl o' Hell'.

Many Scots believe in the Devil and have a great respect for him. Even John Knox, the father of the Reformation Church, admitted that he had once had a conversation with the Devil in the cathedral churchyard in St Andrews.

Devil's Picture Book The *Covenanters* gave this name to playing cards.

Cards are often used for *fortune telling* in Scotland where to turn up the ace of spades means a *death*.

The nine of diamonds is also an unlucky card with a lot of folklore attached to it. One story tells that Sir John Dalrymple of Stair wrote his instructions for the massacre of *Glencoe* to go ahead on the card. Another story tells of how the *'Bloody Butcher'* used it to authorize a death warrant just before the Battle of *Culloden*.

Some people say that the name for the card, 'the Curse of Scotland', stems from the failed attempt of a man trying to steal the Scottish crown. He supposedly only got away with nine diamonds, the value of which was replaced by a swingeing tax on the Scots people.

Devil's Pledge In Orkney it is said that you can pledge yourself to the *Devil* by placing your right hand under the sole of your left foot and putting your left hand on the top of your head.

Dragons of Ben Vehir The mountain at the base of *Glencoe* is called Ben Vehir. (Gaelic *beithir* – a large serpent.) It got this name from a dragon which lived in a cave in the mountain directly above Ballachulish Pier.

Everyone was terrified of this dragon, which terrorized the neighbourhood, tearing people to pieces and eating them; so, one day, a sailor decided to try to destroy her. He anchored his boat a good distance out from the pier and formed a bridge between it and the boat with empty barrels tied together with rope. The barrels were studded with iron spikes. When the bridge was ready he lit a fire on his boat and started to roast some meat. As soon as the dragon smelled the meat she ran down to the shore and started to cross over to the boat. However, the spikes tore her to pieces before she reached the end of the bridge. In the meantime, the sailor moved his boat away from the end of the barrel bridge so that when the dragon reached the end of the bridge she had nowhere to go except into the water where she drowned.

The people who lived in Ballachulish felt safe then, but they did not know that the dragon had given birth to a baby just before she had come down from her cave. In time this dragon also had young which she hid in a haystack on a farm at the foot of the mountain. One day they were discovered by the farmer when setting fire to the stack. The sound of the shrieks of the young dragons burning were blown up the mountain to their mother who rushed down to try to save them. But she was too late, the young dragons were burnt to death. When she saw this the mother lay down on a flat rock near the shore and lashed at the rock with her tail until she died. This rock is called Dragon Rock.

E

Eagle It is said that a golden eagle was seen circling above the ship which brought *Bonnie Prince Charlie* to Scotland as she lay offshore the night before Charles was to take his first step on Scottish soil. Tullibardine, one of the *Seven Men of Moidart*, saw the eagle as a good omen – the king of birds come to welcome Charles on his arrival in Scotland.

Easter Easter Sunday is the first Sunday after the full moon that occurs on the day of the vernal equinox (21 March) or on any of the next twenty-eight days. The 21 March was originally a Celtic festival which, like many pre-Christian celebrations, was adopted into the Christian Church calendar.

The Easter egg, a symbol of the renewal of life which derives from the ancient world, was also taken by the Church and said to symbolize the resurrection. Coloured hard-boiled eggs are rolled by children on Easter Sunday.

Elder (*Sambucus nigra*) There are many *super-stitions* regarding this tree, which supposedly supplied the wood for the Cross. Legend says that Judas Iscariot hanged himself on an elder and a fungus which commonly grows on the bark is called Judas's Ears.

In Scotland the tree is thought to have good properties and it is believed that its bark provides a cure for *warts* and eye ailments. Not only that, it protects people against witchcraft. Strangely, the following recipe for a very refreshing drink was given to the author by a *witch*:

Loosely fill a 1-gallon bucket (4.5 litres) with clean elder flowers without the stems. Add the rind of 3 lemons. Pour 1 gallon (4.5 litres) of boiling water over the flowers and add the juice of the 3 lemons. When the water has cooled to lukewarm, sprinkle 1 ounce (25 g) of yeast on top. Cover with a clean cloth and leave for four days before straining. Leave to stand, covered with a cloth, for three weeks before bottling. Bottles should be corked loosely otherwise they could explode.

Elf A supernatural being which looks like a small human. They are generally more malignant than fairies though the elf queen who took *Thomas the Rhymer* to Elfland gave him the power of sooth-saying on his release.

F

Fairs

> For ye can see them a',
> The lads o' the fair,
> Lads o' the Forth and the Carron water,
> Workin' lads and lads wi' gear,
> Lads wha'll sell ye the Provost's daughter;
> Soldiers back frae the German wars,
> Pedlars up frae the border,
> And lassies wi' an eye for mair than the kye,
> At the Trystin' Fair at Falkirk

gear – harness; *mair* – more; *kye* – cattle

Many of the big markets of former days were held at the time of Church festivals, having been started by the monks who wanted to sell pardons and holy artefacts. By the nineteenth century, however, there was little which was holy left at the fairs, apart from the names of some of them – Edinburgh's All Hallows Fair, which commenced on 1 November, or St Lawrence's Fair (called Lowrin Fair) in the north-east.

Most fairs lasted from three to four days and offered the chance to buy livestock and household goods, clothes and shoes. Sweets, roast chestnuts, gingerbread and other confectionery were on sale and, of course, there was drink. Fiddlers played for dancing and competitions were sometimes organized. Crieff, being situated at the meeting point of the Grampians and the Perthshire hills, was the most important cattle fair well into the eighteenth century when it was superseded by Falkirk.

An event which took place in most market towns on *Quarter-days* was the hiring fair. At this fair

45

domestic and farm workers seeking employment stood in rows to be inspected by people who were looking for labour. Though some people put themselves up for hire at the Market Fairs, only the Hiring Fairs were legalized by statute as true employment exchanges. The fairs declined in the nineteenth century for a variety of reasons and most are only remembered today as dates on the calendar.

Fairy A supernatural being who can change shape. These are nothing like the fairies who are seen on Christmas trees – they are sometimes very ugly. Often called 'the good people', they usually *are* good-natured, though they can also be quite nasty if they do not get their own way as the following traditional story shows.

The Twa Humpy-Backit Laddies
(The two hunch-back boys)

Once upon a time there lived twa humpy-backit laddies. Donald had a hump on his left shoulder and Davie had a hump on his right shoulder. They were both in love with Mary, a very bonnie lassie who lived in the village. They both knew that they had no chance to court her, because they were humpy-backit.

One day Donald went for a walk in the woods. He was thinking about Mary, and he was very depressed. All of a sudden as he was passing a hill he heard some voices singing, 'Monday, Tuesday. Monday, Tuesday.' 'That's no' very interesting,' thought Donald, so he added a bit tail on the end: 'Monday, Tuesday, Wednesday'.

All of a sudden a door in the side of the hill flew open and there in front of Donald stood a host of fairy folk. They were affa ugly. Some o' them was fat, and some o' them was affa thin. Most of all they had the ugliest, ugliest faces. Really horrible they were.

Anyway, one o' them stepped forward and he was the king of these fairy folk. He said, 'Was that you singing just now?'

'Yes, it was,' said Donald. 'What of it? I heard you singing "Monday, Tuesday" and I thought that it wasnae very interesting so I just added a bit tail tae it.'

'Oh, that's just marvellous,' said the king of the fairies. 'You know, we're not very creative and we've been sitting under that hill now for two or three thousand years, give or take a hundred years or so, and always the same song. Anyway, now you've put a nice bit tail to it and made it an affa lot better. Can we do anything for you? Grant you a wish, or anything?'

Well, you know what Donald asked for, of course, that his hump should be taken away.

'No sooner said than done!' said the king.

And there stood Donald, strong and straight and handsome. He didn't stop to say goodbye to the fairies, no, but off he went racing down to the village to see if he could find Mary.

Well – who should he meet on the way but Davie. 'What, in the name . . .?' he began.

But Donald didn't stop. 'I was up the wood,' he shouted and on he went.

'Well,' thought Davie, '"up the wood", eh? I'd better get up the wood myself and see what's been going on.' So off he went. And as he passed the hill he heard the song, 'Monday, Tuesday, Wednesday'.

'That's no' very interesting,' thought Davie and started to sing 'Monday, Tuesday, Wednesday. Thursday, Friday, Saturday. And Sunday. And Sunday.' No sooner were the words out of his mouth than the door in the hill flew open again. But this time the fairy folk came out very angry.

'What's that you're singing?' shouted the fairy king.

'Well, I just thought I'd . . .' started Davie.

'Don't you just think anything,' said the king. 'Do you know, my folk were singing the same song for two-three thousand years and getting on just fine, then along comes a young man – very nice young man he was – and gave us a wee bit tail to our song. Now we're just settling down to learn that and you come along and confuse us all. Do

47

you know what I'm just thinking? We've got a spare hump here in our hill and you can have it for your interfering!' And so saying, he put the second hump on poor Davie's back.

Now Davie is so bowed down with his *twa* humps that his nose trails along the ground and could even be used as a plough if he wanted.

a bonnie lassie – a pretty girl; *fed up* – miserable; *no'* – not; *affa* – awful; *o'* – of; *wasnae* – was not; *tae* – to; *a wee bit tail* – a short ending

This story is told as a moral to remind people what can happen if they stick their noses into other people's business.

Fairy Arrows Prehistoric flint arrow heads are often taken to be fairy arrows or 'elfshot'. There was a belief among some Scots that lumbago and sciatica were caused by 'elfshot'.
(See *Elf.*)

Fairy Knolls Hills where fairies live. If anyone is invited into a *fairy* knoll, he must stick an *iron* blade in the door-frame to keep the door open. If he does not, and the door closes behind him, he can be in the fairy knoll for ages without knowing it. Numerous stories and *ballads* tell of people who have danced with the fairies for what they thought was only a few hours, when in reality they were dancing for a year and a day.

Fairy Rings The circles of darker grass which often appear on lawns are thought to be places where fairies have been dancing. They are, in fact, caused by fungus, the spawn of which radiates outwards in a circle. The darker colour is due to nitrogen coming off the spores. On the plain at Carterhaugh, which is situated where the Ettrick and the Yarrow meet about a mile north of Selkirk, there are two or three rings where grass never grows. People say that these are fairy rings which survive from the time that Tam Lin, the hero of *Child Ballad* 39 was taken away by the *fairy* queen.

Fiery Cross

> Woe to the wretch who fails to rear
> At this dread sign the ready spear!
>> Sir Walter Scott

A light wooden cross with its ends dipped in the blood of a sacrificially slain goat was carried through the glens by teams of fast runners when the *clan* chiefs wanted to rally their men. The fiery cross had the alternative name of the Cross of Shame, for those who disobeyed the call were considered very disloyal. In his poem 'The Lady of the Lake' Sir Walter *Scott* paints a colourful picture of a summons by the fiery cross.

Fifteen, the Name given to the first *Jacobite* rebellion which took place in 1715.
   (See *Old Pretender* and *Forty-five*.)

Fire Many people believe that a fire will not light in direct sunlight, an idea which stems from the belief that fire was originally stolen from the sun. Because of its association with sun-worship, there are many *superstitions* connected with it. It is thought to be unlucky for anyone but a member of the family to poke the fire and if the fire draws badly, it means that there is some evil in the house. This can only be got rid of by placing the poker at right angles to the grate to form the shape of a cross.
   A fire can also be used for *fortune telling*. If the fire burns on only one side of the grate, then a *wedding* will soon take place. Sparks at the back of the fire mean that an important letter is on the way. Oblong cinders are called 'coffins' and indicate a *death* in the family and oval-shaped cinders, called 'cradles', herald a *birth*.

Fire Festivals The old *bonfires* which were lit on Midsummer's Day and *Hallowe'en* in honour of the sun are not even a memory now in most parts of Scotland. The ancient pagan festival of the summer solstice fell on 21 June and was celebrated with huge bonfires which were lit on the hilltops. Young people leapt through the flames for *luck* and cattle were driven over the dying embers to protect them against disease. The ashes of the bonfires were spread over the fields to increase crop fertility.

The bonfires which once blazed on Hallowe'en are now lit on 5 November to commemorate the failure of the Gunpowder Plot in 1605. On this date a number of Roman Catholics, led by Guy Fawkes, tried to blow up the Houses of Parliament in an attempt to get rid of James VI and I. For some days before 5 November, children go round the houses asking if householders have any old wood or furniture for the 'boney' (bonfire). They make a 'Guy' (a figure) out of old clothes stuffed with paper or straw, and wheel him about asking for 'a penny for the guy' which they use to buy fireworks. On the day of the bonfire the guy is burned and the fireworks are let off.

> Please to remember the fifth of November,
> Gunpowder, treason and plot.
> I see no reason why gunpowder treason
> Should ever be forgot.

First-footing There are many rituals and *superstitions* connected with *Hogmanay* (New Year's Eve) in Scotland. One of the most important concerns the 'first-foot', the first person to cross the threshold after 12 midnight on 31 December. This should be a tall, dark, handsome man, carrying gifts for the house, including coal – a symbol of light and warmth; something to drink (usually whisky); salt – for *luck*; and something to eat, often a tin of shortbread. Once in the house, the first-foot puts his gifts on the table and receives a 'nip' (glass of whisky) and some black bun (fruit cake).

A good first-foot brings luck to the people in the house, but if something goes wrong and an unlucky person crosses the threshold first, then the occupants of the house will have bad luck for the following year. A woman, particularly if she is a red-head, is considered very unlucky.

Flodden – The Flowers of the Forest

I've heard them lilting, at the ewe milking,
Lasses a-lilting, before the dawn of day;
But now they are moaning, on ilka green
loaning;
The flowers of the forest are a' wede awae.

ilka – every; *loaning* – milking park; *wede awae* – vanished

Many tales are related about the awful Battle of Flodden (1513) which resulted in a massive defeat for Scotland by the English. One legend tells that the night before the battle ghostly heralds stood at the Mercat Cross in Edinburgh and read out a list of the 10000 men who were to die the next day. An Edinburgh man called Richard Lawson was walking up the High Street when the sky turned scarlet. He heard the list read out, beginning with the name of the king. When his own name was read out he fell to his knees and prayed that he would not be killed. Obviously his prayer was answered for he was the only man mentioned on the list who survived the battle.

'The Flowers of the Forest' was written by Jane Elliot (1727–1805) to lament the deaths of over 10000 Scotsmen, among them King James IV.

51

There is a *superstition* among some folk-singers that to sing 'The Flowers of the Forest' will result in a death. For this reason it is usually only played or sung at *funerals*.

Flowers As in every country there is a wealth of folklore attached to flowers. Scots gardeners say that if there are more than twelve daisies on your lawn, then spring has arrived. Flowers and other seeds planted at the time of the new moon are believed to grow best.

Red roses are a token of love but you should never give a bunch made up of red and white flowers to anyone in Scotland. The two colours together denote 'blood and bandages' and are considered particularly unlucky.

Country people believe that bad luck will befall anyone who takes flowers which have bloomed out of season into a house and 'Dead Man's Florrel' (cowbane – *cicuta virosa*) should *never* be taken indoors as it will cause death. There may be something in this last *superstition* as the plant contains a highly poisonous substance, cicutoxin, in all its parts.

Folk Festivals The dozen or so folk festivals which take place all over Scotland throughout the year are a result of the folk-music revival which encouraged so many folk clubs to spring up in the fifties.

One of the earliest festivals at Blairgowrie, started by the Traditional Music and Song Association (formed in 1965), was intended to bring traditional musicians and enthusiasts together. Blairgowrie was followed by annual festivals at Kinross, Newcastleton and Keith. Glenfarg and Carrbridge folk festivals were started in the late seventies and Auchtermuchty celebrated the tenth anniversary of its festival in August 1990. This last, like the Girvan Festival, takes place over a weekend. So much is packed into this short time – singing and story-telling competitions, community events, *ceilidhs* and informal sessions – that it could well be extended to last a week.

The relatively new Paisley Festival, held annually in the last week in May, incorporates folk-music concerts with writers' weekends, community theatre, historical walks and a host of events for children. Amateurs and professionals work hand in hand to make this one of the most interesting and varied folk festivals in Scotland. The Edinburgh International Folk Festival, a ten-day event taking place every Easter, was started in 1978. As suggested by its title, Edinburgh attracts both national and international talent. Glasgow's Mayfest is a Celtic celebration, attracting the best of Irish, Bretonic and Scots performers. In 1990 Glasgow was the European City of Culture, celebrating with 365 days of national and international music, theatre and art which was enjoyed by local and foreign visitors alike.

Folk-music The traditional music of the people of Scotland is very much alive with over fifty folk clubs and live music in pubs. Concerts and radio programmes can be heard regularly and *folk festivals* take place all over Scotland throughout the year.

Since the start of the folk-song revival in the fifties, many interesting groups and singer-songwriters have sprung up. The resulting mixture of music which can be heard in Scotland today ranges from interpreters of traditional song, including Jack Beck and Heather Heywood, through the folk-rock of the Tannahill Weavers, Tonight at Noon and Silly Wizard, and the folk-jazz of the Easy Club to the 'fusion' music of Hamish Moore and Dick Lee, who bring together the sound of the *bagpipes* with the saxophone. Themes covered by singer-songwriters like Dick Gaughan and Iain MacDonald include national and international politics, while Archie Fisher and Eric Bogle, the latter now living in Australia, explore cultural and personal identity.

The *School of Scottish Studies* has also produced and documented a series of records and cassettes from their unique archive recordings. Covering many aspects of Scots and Gaelic traditional music and folklore, each record comes with a substantial booklet containing detailed descriptive notes and illustrations, together with transcriptions and translations of the texts. The School also publishes the magazine *Tocher*, which contains material selected from the archives, including stories and songs.

Forty-five, the *Jacobite* rebellion which took place in 1745 in an attempt to place *Bonnie Prince Charlie* on the throne.

(See also the *Fifteen* and the *Old Pretender*.)

Fortune Telling The art of fortune telling is often passed on from parent to child and people who have this gift are said to have *second sight*.

Many fortune tellers work at *fairs*, telling fortunes in various ways, but always only on the condition that their palms are crossed with silver. Some do the prediction with cards, often using Tarot cards, while others read hands. Fortune tellers say that the right hand is what your parents give you, the left hand is what you make of yourself. Reading tea-leaves is also popular amongst 'spey-wives' (fortune tellers).

To prepare a cup for a reading, swirl the last of the tea around in a clockwise direction and wish or think about what you want to know before inverting the cup over the saucer. The tea leaves should be left sticking inside the cup. The fortune teller can then 'read' the tea leaves by interpreting the shapes that they have made. Tea leaves towards the top of the cup represent things that are going to happen soon, those towards the bottom may happen later.

People who tell fortunes often seem to be quite uncanny. However, through constant dealings with different people fortune tellers acquire the ability to sum up their subjects very quickly. An old book on gypsy-lore lists a number of statements which fortune tellers can always use to be certain of hitting the target with their customers. Among these are: that something of great advantage will come the way of the subject very soon;

that they have an enemy; and that they once got into trouble by doing a good deed.

(See *Thomas the Rhymer*.)

Four Maries When *Mary Queen of Scots* was sent to France in 1548 she was accompanied by four companions, also called Mary – Mary Fleming, Mary Beaton, Mary Livingston and Mary Seton. Many *ballads* and songs were written about the queen's Maries as well as about life at court at that time. One song which is still sung today, the ballad of Mary *Hamilton*, thought to be about another companion of the queen, is probably a mixture of stories about two different people.

Friar of Ayr's Blessing The Church in Scotland played a prominent part in the country's War of Independence (1296–1328), not only in keeping the spirit of resistance alive by preaching, but also by fighting physically with the *Auld Enemy*. After the *Black Parliament* at Ayr, *Wallace* managed to kill a vast number of English soldiers. Some other English soldiers, who had been quartered in a nearby monastery, had eluded him, however. When the prior of the monastery heard that Wallace and his men had been lured into a trap by Edward, the *'Hammer of the Scots'* and that some of the Scots had been hanged, he got his monks to kill the English soldiers. The people called the massacre the 'Friar of Ayr's Blessing'.

Funerals A great deal of ritual is connected with funerals in every country. Most Scottish funerals are followed by a meal or a drink and a snack, a custom which harks back to the old 'wakes', which took the form of prayers and mourning combined with eating and drinking.

In some parts of Scotland it is still common for members of the family to sit with a corpse the night before the funeral, the corpse surrounded by candles to keep evil spirits away, and the practice of touching a corpse to prevent haunting is also continued by some Scots. The custom of burying people with their feet and face towards the east is a relic of sun-worship, though this has been adopted by the Christian Church which says that the summons to the Last Judgment will come from that direction.

Superstition says that a corpse which does not stiffen up is waiting for another *death* and that if the sun shines brightly on the face of one of the mourners at the graveside, then he will be the next to die.

G

George I

> Came ye o'er frae France?
> Came ye doon by Lunnon?
> Saw ye Geordie Whelps,
> And his bonny woman?
> Were ye at the place
> Ca'd the Kittle Hoosie?
> Saw ye Geordie's grace
> Riding on a goosie?

George Ludwig Kurfürst von Hannover, who was a very unpopular monarch, ascended the British throne in 1714 as a result of an Act of Parliament designed to ensure that no Roman Catholic monarch should reign in Britain. George was fat and never learned to speak proper English – two of many faults which provided Scots caricaturists and lampooners with plenty to make fun of. He also brought his German mistresses to court with him.

In the song 'Came Ye O'er Frae France' the 'goosie' is Duchess Schulenburg to whom George had given the title Duchess of Kendal. The song appeared in James Hogg's collection of Jacobite songs in 1819, but a version of it was already being sung in 'Geordie's' time.

The word 'Whelps' is a corruption of 'Guelph', the dynasty which ruled Hanover until 1866. The present British royal family is descended from them.

Ghosts

> You crave one kiss of my clay-cold lips;
> But my breath smells earthy strong;
> If you have one kiss of my clay-cold lips,
> Your time will not be long.

Ghosts and ghost stories abound in Scottish folklore. Many people believe that anyone who has met a violent death will walk as a ghost until his soul is put to rest somehow. Children who die unbaptized are also thought to wander as ghosts in lonely places. Many Scottish *ballads* tell of ghosts visiting lovers whom they have left behind. These ghosts must leave before cock crow and always warn their lovers not to kiss them.

Glasgow Flourish The motto on the coat of arms of the city of Glasgow. It is an abbreviation of 'Lord, let Glasgow flourish through the preaching of thy word and praising of thy Name.' Though the coat of arms was first authorized as late as October 1866, the heraldic motifs it bears appear in seals of the early bishops of Glasgow as well as in the burgh arms in the sixteenth century. These motifs, an oak tree, bird, fish and bell, relate to stories about *St Kentigern* who founded a cathedral on the site now occupied by Glasgow Cathedral.
(See the *Tree That Never Grew.*)

Glencoe – The Vale of Tears

> Oh, cold is the snow that drapes Glencoe,
> And covers the grave o' Donald.
> And cruel was the foe that raped Glencoe,
> And murdered the house of MacDonald.

In 1691 all the chiefs of the *clans* were forced to renounce their allegiance to James VII and pledge themselves to William III. William had offered a pardon to those chiefs who would swear loyalty to him before 31 December, but Maclain, chief of the clan MacDonald, delayed to the last minute, only setting out for Fort William at the end of December. Arriving at Fort William in a blizzard, Maclain was told that he must go to Inverary to swear his oath. Accordingly, he travelled on, and took the oath there on 6 January.

The MacDonalds were not loved by the authorities: they were Catholics and also *Jacobites*. They were also notorious thieves and robbers. The magistrates therefore decided to take the opportunity of old Maclain's late registration to punish the whole clan.

Sir John Dalrymple, Secretary of State for Scotland, wrote to the commander-in-chief of Scotland on 11 January 1691. '. . . Glencoe hath not taken the oaths; at which I rejoice – it's a great work of charity to be exact in rooting out that damnable sect . . .'

At the beginning of February a detachment of 120 men of the Earl of Argyll's regiment set out from Inverlochy under the command of Campbell of Glenlyon, a relative by marriage of Maclain. The Campbells accepted hospitality from the Mac-Donalds, staying with them for twelve days. But at 5.00 a.m. on the morning of 13 February they rose to murder thirty-eight of their hosts. When the Campbells left Glencoe they took with them 200 horses, 900 cattle and many sheep and goats. Their orders had been to kill everyone under seventy years of age and to make especially sure that Maclain and all the members of his family died. No mention was made of the incident at the next sitting of the Scots parliament, and the Mac-Donalds and the Campbells became sworn enemies as a result of the massacre.

(See *Devil's Picture Book*.)

Granite City The city of Aberdeen is so called because its buildings are made of granite. Until oil was discovered, Aberdeen was mainly a fishing port, and as such was a great source of whaling and other fishing songs. Since the discovery of oil and the influx of Americans into the area, Aberdonian music has taken on a decidedly country and western flavour.

Green Almost every colour has at least one *superstition* attached to it in Scotland but perhaps green, being a *fairy* colour, has the most. According to Scots folklore, anyone wearing green runs the risk of being taken away by the fairies. It is the colour of envy and jealousy, not just among the fairy folk, but among mortals, too. It is considered very unlucky to get married in green and if an actor or actress wears green on stage it will bring misfortune to the play and the actors.

Greyfriars Bobby At the top of Edinburgh's Candle-maker Row at its junction with George IV Bridge stands the statue of a little Skye terrier – Bobby.

In 1858 Bobby was the constant companion of 'Auld Jock' Gray. After Gray died and had been buried in Greyfriars Kirkyard, Bobby stood guard over his grave and for fourteen years the faithful little dog refused to be chased away from his master's last resting-place. Mr John Traill of the Greyfriars Dining Rooms (now Greyfriars Bobby Bar) and Mr Brown, the caretaker of Greyfriars Kirk, fed him and he became well known to the children in the neighbouring Heriot's Hospital, endowed by *Jinglin' Geordie*.

In 1867 the Lord Provost, William Chambers, co-founder of the Chambers publishing house, made Bobby a freeman of the city of Edinburgh.

The statue to Bobby was set up in 1872 on the instructions of Baroness Burdett-Coutts to com-memorate the faithfulness of the dog who had slept on his master's grave, winter and summer, for fourteen years. Originally a drinking fountain with two basins, one at ground level for passing dogs, the lower fountain is now dry and the upper one has been filled in.

Bobby's collar, and other things connected with him, can be seen in Edinburgh's Huntly House Museum.

H

Haggis is a man-made delicacy, Scotland's national dish. A recipe in an old cookery book suggests taking the stomach of a sheep, washing it well, turning it inside out, scalding it in boiling water and then scraping it quickly with a knife. This bag is then filled with a mixture of sheep's heart, liver, windpipe and lights mixed with the sheep's blood, salt, and a lot of pepper. All this is boiled in a big pot for about four hours. The windpipe is left draining over the edge of the pot 'to drain off impurities'.

Haggis can be bought ready-made and, if you do not think about what has gone into it, makes a very tasty dish. To cook, prick the haggis once or twice with a skewer then put it into a pot of gently simmering water for about one hour. Drained and served with 'clapshot' (boiled potato and turnip mashed together) it makes a good filling meal for a cold winter's evening.

Hallowe'en All Hallows Eve. The last day of the year in the old Celtic calendar was 31 October and so a very important date in Scotland. Scots children love Hallowe'en, when they play a lot of games and 'dook' (duck) for apples. A large basin is filled with cold water and nuts and apples are floated in it. One or two players at a time get down on their knees with their hands behind their backs to try to lift the apples out with their teeth. Some people put coins in the water which, of course, sink to the bottom. Brave dookers can get the coins only if they are prepared to put their heads right under the water. Eating a treacle scone tied to bit of string is also a favourite – before the scones are eaten everyone is covered in treacle.

Witches are said to fly at Hallowe'en and turnip lanterns are made to scare any *witch* who may be lurking round the doors. To make a 'tumshie' (turnip lantern) you cut the top off a quite big turnip and scoop out the inside of the bottom bit. You can use a spoon or a knife for this. Now you have a shell in which you cut holes for eyes, a nose and mouth. Some children put matchsticks in the mouth to look like teeth. A candle is fixed inside so that its light shines out through the holes and a string is tied through the sides so that the tumshie can be hung on a stick. The turnip that is scooped out is usually cooked and mashed up with potatoes to make 'clapshot'. Lucky charms and money are mixed into it – the money brings good *luck* and the lucky charms are used for *fortune telling* divinations.

Hamilton, Mary *Child Ballad* No. 173

> Word is to the kitchen gone
> And word is to the hall,
> And word is up to Madam the Queen
> And that's the worst of all,
> That Mary Hamilton's borne a babe
> To the highest Stuart of all.

Child suggests that this ballad is a compilation of two separate historical occurrences. The first took place at the court of *Mary Queen of Scots* when a French woman gave birth to an illegitimate child whose father was the court apothecary. Both parents murdered the baby and were later hanged in Edinburgh.

In the second case, some two centuries later, a remarkably beautiful Scots woman – Mary Hamilton – who was maid-of-honour to the Empress Catherine of Russia, had an affair with a handsome aide-de-camp of the tzar. The body of a child was found in a well and Mary Hamilton admitted that she was the mother, confessing not only to having killed that child, but also two other unwanted children. She was sent to Petropaulovsk fortress where she was condemned to death on 27

November 1718 and executed on 14 March the following year. Mary went to her execution dressed in white with black ribbons, hoping to excite the sympathy of the tzar. However, he ordered the executioner to get on with his work and Mary's head was cut off. It is said that the beautiful head was preserved in spirits and kept for sixty years or so at the Academy of Sciences in St Petersburg.

Over the years the story from the Stuart court has mingled with that from Russia, the father of the child developing into 'the highest Stuart of all' i.e. Darnley, the husband of Mary Queen of Scots.

Hammer of the Scots The name for Edward I (1239–1307), so called because he repeatedly tried to conquer Scotland. He is buried in Westminster Abbey where the inscription on his tombstone reads: 'Edwardus Primus Malleus Scotorum hic est' (Edward I – Hammer of the Scots). He was also nicknamed 'Longshanks' because he had very long legs.

(See *Bruce; Friar of Ayr's Blessing; Heart of Bruce.*)

Heart of Bruce As Robert the *Bruce* lay dying of leprosy in Cardoss Castle on 7 June 1329, he asked his friend Sir James Douglas to carry his heart to Jerusalem. Bruce hoped that with this act God would forgive him for not having kept his vow to go on the Crusades, which he had been unable to do on account of his war against England. Sir James agreed and after Bruce's death the heart was embalmed and put into a silver case which was hung round Douglas's neck on a chain. Douglas set off for the Holy Land travelling via Spain, but when he got there he found the Spaniards at war with the Moors. Staying to fight the Saracens he rode into battle with the casket containing the heart still round his neck but, suddenly finding himself surrounded by Moors, he tore off the casket and flung it in amongst them shouting, 'Pass on as thou wert wont; I will follow or die!' He was immediately struck down and after the battle his dead body was found lying over Bruce's heart. Friends took his body home for burial in the church of St Bride in Douglas, Isle of Man, and Bruce's heart was entrusted to Sir Simon Locard of Lee who took it back to Scotland for burial under the altar in Melrose Abbey. Sir Simon changed his name afterwards to Lockheart (modern spelling Lockhart).

Strangely enough, the sworn enemy of Bruce, Edward I, the *'Hammer of the Scots'*, also asked on his deathbed that his heart, too, be conveyed to the Holy Land. He had fought in Jerusalem and had sworn to return there but never did because of his war with Scotland. Edward's heart did not reach the Holy Land either, for the money for the expedition to take it there was squandered. In *The Book of Days, Chambers* remarks that if the wishes of Bruce and Edward had been fulfilled 'the hearts of these two inveterate enemies would have met to rest quietly together for ever, in the same sepulchre'.

The heart of John *Baliol,* another Scotsman who was closely linked with Bruce and Edward, was embalmed by his widow and enclosed in an ivory casket enamelled with silver. Widow Baliol had this casket placed on her table every time she took a meal and when she died she had it placed on her own heart in her tomb. She was buried in 1289 near the altar in New Abbey, Galloway, which received the new name of Dolce Cor (Sweetheart Abbey).

Heart of Midlothian A heart-shaped set of stones in Edinburgh's High Street. It marks the place where the old Tolbooth, one of Edinburgh's prisons, used to stand. The Tolbooth was demolished in 1817.

Henwife A good *witch.* Very often an old woman who keeps a few hens, she helps people to overcome their difficulties.

Hogmanay 31 December, being one of the feast days in the Celtic calendar, is very important for

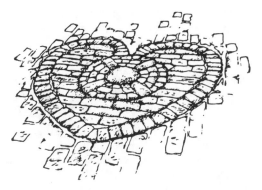

the Scots. It is on this day that the Old Year dies and the New Year begins. Many *superstitions* are connected with Hogmanay, for example, *first-footing*.

The Scots believe that the first person to cross the threshold on 1 January determines the luck of the house and its occupants for the whole year. The first-foot should be a tall, dark, handsome man carrying gifts for the people of the house, including salt, bread, and, of course, some whisky. After a family has been first-footed they often visit other houses to first-foot their friends, collecting more and more people as they go. In Edinburgh it is usual to meet at about 11.00 p.m. at the Tron Kirk and go first-footing from there. At the end of a long Hogmanay night and the beginning of New Year's Day many Scots can be seen straggling home with sore heads, happy that they have 'seen in the New Year' properly.

Holly A folk tradition which Scotland shares with many other countries says that branches from this plant made the crown of thorns which Christ wore when he was crucified. The berries, which were once white, were stained with his blood. It is considered very bad in Scotland to burn holly, and to step on the holly berries and crush them will bring bad *luck*.
(See Robin Redbreast.)

Horseman's Word '. . . if I fail to keep these promises may my flesh be torn to pieces with a wild horse . . .'

Until the beginning of this century, Scottish ploughmen in the north-east of Scotland were initiated into the fraternity of the horseman's word – a brotherhood linked with the *Devil*, which supposedly gave its members great power over horses.

Candidates, chosen from young ploughmen, were sometimes sent a horsehair through the post as a sign that they had been elected to join the horsemen. Others were simply told, often outside the church after Sunday service, that they were to be initiated. The initiation ceremony was performed in a darkened cowshed where, among other things, the candidate had to 'shake hands with the Devil', usually the cloven hoof of a calf. The ceremony was highly secret and anyone speaking to an outsider about what went on could expect dire punishment. Even so, in the early 1900s, one old horseman divulged the secret oath taken at the ceremony. The oath, which includes a colourful account of what will happen to any horseman who discloses the secrets of the horseman's word, may be seen in the Royal Museum of Scotland in Edinburgh.

I

Iona An island off the coast of Mull, Argyllshire, which was the ancient burial place of Scottish kings. Iona was the headquarters of the Church of Scotland until 826, after which it moved to Dunkeld in Perthshire, because of attacks from the Norsemen. The Gaelic name for the island is Ey Colum Cille (the island of the church of St *Columba*) and it is a place of pilgrimage.

Ireland Scots and Irish folklore have a lot in common, especially regarding things supernatural. Both countries share *fairy* legends and some of their mythological heroes. This is not surprising as the Irish and the Scottish Highlanders are basically of the same stock and share the same Gaelic language. St *Columba,* who first brought Christianity to Scotland, was an Irishman, as was Fergus, who is accredited with bringing the *Stone of Destiny* with him when he founded *Dalriada* with his brothers.
(See *Iona, Scotia.)*

Iron Iron counters *fairy* magic and a drawn sword offers special protection. Humans very often put a dagger or a knife into the door-frame of a *fairy knoll* to keep the door open. Iron thresholds were often incorporated into houses as protection against evil and, though none are known to remain today in Scotland, two such thresholds still exist in England. An iron knife was often placed in the bed when a woman was giving *birth* to avoid the fairies taking her or the baby and the child had a pin stuck in its bonnet for protection until it was baptized. Horseshoes still remain a symbol of good *luck* in Scotland and are often given to a bride at her *wedding.*
(See *Baptism, Changeling.)*

J

Jack A favourite of the *travelling people,* Jack is a kind of trickster figure who often appears in folk-tales. Like all tricksters or fools, Jack represents good sense.

One story tells how Jack's mother was about to die. Very unhappy, Jack went for a walk on the seashore. As he was walking, he met Death, his scythe over his shoulder, coming for Jack's mother. Furious with rage, Jack fought with Death, smashed him up with his own scythe and stuffed the broken pieces of Death's body into a nutshell which he threw far out to sea.

Jack felt marvellous and ran home to find his mother up and about and felling quite well. 'I've conquered Death,' thought Jack. 'He'll never bother my mother – or anybody else, for that matter – again.' But he said nothing to his mother about what he had done.

The two sat down to have some breakfast, but when they tried to cook some eggs the shells would not break. Try as they might, there was no way that they could break the eggshells. Later in the day, Jack's mother asked him to kill a cockerel so that she could make some soup. He tried everything but the cockerel would not die. And so it went on – from day to day, all over the world, nothing could be killed and nothing would die. Jack had destroyed Death and, without him, life went on for ever.

When Jack realized what he had done he told his mother. 'Oh, Jack,' said his mother, 'you've done a terrible thing: you've destroyed the only thing which keeps the world alive. Without Death there is no life.'

'But I only did it for you, Mother,' said Jack.

'Well,' said his mother, 'do something else for me – find that nutshell and set Death free.'

Jack hurried off but after walking for miles and miles along the shore he still had not found the nut. 'How can I ever find that nut again?' he thought, and sat down on a rock in despair. Suddenly, there at his feet, he saw the nutshell bobbing in the water. He scooped it up and let Death out.

'Well, Jack, are you happy?' asked Death.

'No, I am not,' mumbled Jack.

'You've got a lot to learn, Jack,' said Death, 'but now you know that without me there is no life.'

Jacobites The name given to the supporters of James (Jacobus) Stuart who was deposed in 1688. In 1714 they rose again in support of the *Old Pretender* and were responsible for the rising in 1715 which resulted in the battles of Preston and Sherrifmuir. With the death of *Chevalier* James they transferred their allegiance to his son, *Bonnie Prince Charlie*, but after initial success at Prestonpans in 1745, they were finally defeated a year later at *Culloden*.

(See Bloody Butcher, Sir John Cope.)

Jacobite Alphabet The *Jacobites,* loyal to James VII, the *Old Pretender* and to *Bonnie Prince Charlie,* used the letters of the alphabet to give voice to their secret feelings as follows:

ABC – A Blessed Change (out with the Hanoverians).
DEF – Damn Every Foreigner, i.e. George I and George II.
GHJ – Get Home James.
KLM – Keep Loyal Ministers.
NOP – No Oppressive Parliaments.
TUW – Turn Up Whelps (the 'Whelps' meant Guelphs, the dynasty which ruled in Hanover until 1866).
XYZ – 'xert Your Zeal.

(See King over the Water.)

Jinglin' Geordie The Edinburgh goldsmith George Heriot, banker and jeweller to James VI, was given the nickname 'Jinglin'' because the sound of gold coins jingling in his pocket always accompanied him as he walked. He endowed Heriot's Hospital for the care and education of 'puir orphan an' faderless boys' around 1700.

As goldsmith to the king, Heriot was a very rich man and many fables grew up about the extent of his wealth. One story goes that Jinglin' Geordie was visiting the king at Holyrood where he remarked on the lovely smell of the smoke from the fire. When the king told him that the wood which was burning was very expensive, Heriot said he would show the king an even more expensive fire in his small shop in Parliament Close. Next day the king visited him, only to find a miserable, ordinary fire. 'Is this it, then?' said the king.

'Wait till I get some more fuel,' said Geordie, and produced a bond for £2000 which he gave the king to put on the fire.

John o' Groats The town of John o' Groats is in the very north of Scotland near Caithness. Legend has it that three Dutch brothers, Gavin, Malcolm and Jan de Groot settled there some centuries ago, building a house. By the sixteenth century eight families bearing the (Scotified) name o' Groat lived there. One time when the families met together for a celebration a quarrel arose as to who should come into the house first and sit at the head of the table. John o' Groat solved the problem by building an eight-sided room with eight doors and containing an octagonal table.

K

Kelpies Water-horses which live in salt water. They are very big, have beards, big mouths and flat noses. Their smaller relations, the glashans, which are only as big as Shetland ponies, live in freshwater rivers and lochs. Their main source of food is the blood of drowned people. Some people think that the *Loch Ness Monster* is a kelpie.

Kilt The kilt as we know it today is a far cry from the original blanket, dyed with natural dyes, which the Highlanders wrapped around themselves a few centuries ago. Called in Gaelic a *féile-beag (philibeg* – short cover) this was the essential item of dress for the Scottish Highlanders before it was banned in the eighteenth century. It was, in effect, a sort of blanket or 'plaid' which was pinned over the chest with a piece of bone or wood and tied round the middle with a leather belt. Most of the part which hung down from the belt was pleated but about a yard either side was left unpleated. When the wearers were on the move it was easy enough to unwrap the plaid at night and use it as a cover.

In 1746, after the defeat at *Culloden,* the government passed an Act for the 'Abolition and Proscription of the Highland dress' and the Highlanders were forced into trews. When the Act was repealed in 1782, the kilt was still regarded as something only to be worn by the Highland peasants.

Today it is an item of dress more associated with Lowlanders and members of the royal family. The visit of George IV to Edinburgh in 1822, for which Sir Walter *Scott* set up a Highland pantomime with Geordie himself as the kilted star, started off the

71

trend among the upper classes for the garment. The fashion was continued during the Romantic period and reinforced by Queen Victoria and her husband Albert who had a castle built at Balmoral where they could enjoy painting and walking. The kilt became an elegant item of dress, which nowadays can still be seen adorning royal personages.

King's Evil Scrofula or tuberculosis (especially of the lymphatic glands). This disease was thought to be cured by the royal touch. James Stuart, the *Old Pretender* and father of *Bonnie Prince Charlie*, was said to have this power.

King's Fool Archie Armstrong, court jester to James VI and I. He first came to the notice of the king when he landed in court for sheep-stealing. Archie had stolen the sheep, even though he knew the punishment for this was death. When the king's officers came into Archie's hut on the moors he hid the sheep in a cradle and began singing a lullaby to it. The officers searched the hut but found nothing and were just going when one of them asked, 'Is the child a girl or a boy?'

'A dinna ken,' (I don't know) replied Archie.

'It's the sheep,' said the officer and hauled Archie off to the court.

72

Archie was found guilty and condemned to death. As was usual, the king gave him the opportunity to say something before the sentence was carried out. Archie said, 'Take peety on a puir ignoramus Sir King that has haird tell o' the Bible and never read it. For my soul's weal, let me read the Book before I dee.' (Take pity on a poor fool who has heard of the Bible but never read it. For the sake of my soul, let me read it before I die.) When the king granted this request, Archie laughed and said, 'The Diel tak me gin I ever read a word o't as lang as my een are open.' (May the Devil take me if I ever read a word of the Bible as long as my eyes are open.)

The king replied, 'Archie, ye've come to court in Scotland; now ye shall come to court in London, and be my jester till your een be shut.' And so Archie Armstrong became the king's fool.

King over the Water, the The *Jacobites* devised a set of codes to refer to the men they believed should rule Britain. The name 'king over the water' was originally given to James II after his flight to France in 1688 and later used to refer to the *Old Pretender, Bonnie Prince Charlie* and his brother, Henry, Cardinal of York. When the Jacobites appeared to be drinking a toast to King George, they passed their glasses over a jug of water, indicating that they were drinking to 'the king over the water'.

(See *Jacobite Alphabet.*)

Kings Who Never Ruled There is a monument in St Peter's Church in Rome dedicated to James III, Charles III and Henry IX, 'kings of England'. The monument is said to have been erected by King George IV to the *Old Pretender, Bonnie Prince Charlie* and Henry, Cardinal of York who was the brother of Charles. Henry died in 1807, a pensioner of George III.

Kirk of Skulls Gamrie Church in Banffshire is so called because it has the skulls of Norsemen who were killed in battle in a neighbouring field built into its walls.

Knights of the Thistle It is said that King *Achaius,* who ruled at the time of the Emperor Charlemagne, founded the Order of the Knights of the Thistle, consisting of thirteen knights – himself and twelve others – in imitation of Christ and the twelve apostles. Achaius insisted that there should never be more than thirteen knights in the order, but George IV invested more nobles with the order when he visited Scotland in the 1820s. The ornament worn by the Knights of the Thistle is a picture of *St Andrew* with his cross, surrounded by *thistles* and *rue.* The thistle is the emblem of the Scots, rue the emblem of the *Picts.*

L

Lammas In the farming calendar Lammas, which fell on 1 August, was an important *Quarter-day* on which lands which had earlier been let to individual holders were redistributed.

The word 'Lammas' comes from the old English *hlafmæsse* or *hlammæsse* – the loaf-mass. In olden times loaves stamped with a sheaf of corn were taken to the church to be blessed on 1 August, the date on which the harvest season began. The Church of Scotland still has a Harvest Thanksgiving service in autumn to which people bring bread with a wheatsheaf embossed on it, as well as fruit, nuts and other foodstuffs. These things are later distributed amongst old and needy people in the community.

Lia-fàil The Irish name for the *Stone of Destiny*, which was brought to *Dalriada* by Fergus at the beginning of the sixth century.

Little Gentleman in Velvet A *Jacobite* toast to the mole who made the molehill on which William III's horse, Sorrel, stumbled on 21 February 1702. William fell, breaking his collar bone. He died at Kensington two weeks later as a result.

Lion The popular name for William I of Scotland (1143–1214) who chose a red lion rampant (standing on its hind legs) for his standard. The lion is surrounded by a tressure (border) of fleurs-de-lis. In the ninth century Charlemagne granted *Achaius* of Scotland the right to use the French symbol as a token of the friendship cemented in the *Auld Alliance*; Charlemagne decreed that 'The lilies of France should be a defence to the lion of Scotland.'

Loch Ness Monster 'Nessie' was first brought to the attention of the public in an article on 2 May 1933 in which the *Inverness Courier* reported that a well-known local businessman and his wife, driving along the north shore of Loch Ness the previous Friday, had seen an enormous creature, a bit like a whale, rolling and plunging about on the surface of the loch some three-quarters of a mile from the shore. The report carried the headline, 'STRANGE SPECTACLE ON LOCH NESS – WHAT WAS IT?' and though several theories have been put forward since the first sighting, no one really knows.

Some people believe that Nessie is a *kelpie*, others say it is a prehistoric monster or a great orm (sea snake). Many believe that it only appears to those who have drunk enough of a certain well-known local magic potion. However, that some sort of creature is in Loch Ness is generally accepted and scientific teams from all over the world make regular explorations of the loch.

Lousie Lauther This was the name given to Lauder in Berwickshire by people from the surrounding villages. When asked the reason why, Robert *Chambers* received the following answer:

> Deed, I think there's nae muckle need o' proving the matter, for yere ain skins should ken better than I can tell ye; but there's just ae thing I'll swear to, and that is, that nae farer gane than yesterday, as I was commin' owre to the town, I met a Lauder chest o' drawers takin' the road for Edinburgh, o' its ain accord, as hard as it could hotch!

> (Indeed, I don't think the thing needs to be proved because your own skins should tell you the reason why. But one thing, I'll swear to. Yesterday as I was walking towards Lauder I met a chest of drawers taking the road to Edinburgh as fast as it could go.)

Luck Many Scots believe that certain things affect luck. The following bring good luck:

A new **baby** should be given a small sum of money.

If you see a lost **shoe** in the road, kick it and say, 'Kick an old shoe for luck.'

In contrast to many other countries, a **black cat** signifies good luck in Scotland.

A **chimney sweep** usually brings good luck in Scotland but Hughie Clark, who swept the chimneys of Girvan at the turn of the century was considered unlucky. No one knew why, for he was a nice man, but for some reason the people of Girvan thought he was an unlucky sweep.

Horseshoes bring good luck, possibly because they are made of *iron* which helps to ward off evil.

A **four-leafed clover** is supposed to be very lucky. Anyone finding one will increase their luck if they pass it on to someone else. The four-leafed clover was supposedly taken by Eve when she was put out of the Garden of Eden.

Some things which bring bad luck are:

Spilling **salt.** To counteract the bad luck you should throw a pinch of the salt over your left shoulder. People say that the salt goes into the *Devil*'s eyes when you do this.

Combing your **hair** at night. If you do this, a friend will have an accident.

Putting **shoes** on a table. This brings very bad luck as someone may die.

Getting **married in May** is considered very unlucky. The Roman feast of Bona Dea, the goddess of chastity, took place in this month so it is traditionally a time of temperance. On the day that *Mary Queen of Scots* married Darnley in May 1565, someone pinned a note reading, 'Only wantons marry in the month of May' to the door of a house near Holyrood Palace.

(See *Charm, Superstition.*)

Lyon, King of Arms Scotland's chief heraldic officer takes his name from the *lion* on the national standard. He presides over the Lyon Court and deals with questions about armour, coats of arms and precedency.

M

MacCrimmon The MacCrimmon family of Dunvegan in Skye are famous through legend as pipers who were taught their art by the *Devil* or some other supernatural being. One legend tells that the Black Lad MacCrimmon, the youngest of three sons, was the first of them to be given the gift of piping. Every evening, the Black Lad's father used to take down his *bagpipes* (called Black Gate) and play a tune. He then handed it to his eldest son, who would pass it on to the second son. The Black Lad never got a chance to play the pipes. Not only that, he was kept down by the rest in everything and made to do all the hardest work in the house.

One day when old father MacCrimmon and the two brothers had gone out, the Black Lad took a chanter (the pipe with finger holes on which the bagpipe melody is played) and started to play on it. Suddenly a *banshee* from the castle appeared. When she asked him if he would rather have success without skill or skill without success the Black Lad answered without hesitation that he would rather have the latter. Pulling a hair from her head, the banshee told the Black Lad to wind it round the reed of the chanter. She then told him to put his fingers on the holes of the chanter and she put her fingers on top. Together they played a wonderful melody and when they had finished she gave him the name 'King of the Pipers', telling him that no one would equal his skill.

As soon as the banshee had gone the Black Lad took down Black Gate and started to play. There was no tune that he could not play on it and he played and played until his father and brothers came home. As they approached the house they were astonished to hear beautiful music, but as soon as they entered the house, the Black Lad stopped playing. None of them mentioned having heard the music and in the evening the old man took down Black Gate as usual, first playing it himself, then handing it to his eldest, then his second son. When all had finished playing the old man gave the pipes to the Black Lad who played the finest music that had ever been heard.

Macdonald, Flora

> Speed, bonnie boat, like a bird on the wing,
> Onward the sailors cry;
> Carry the lad that's born to be king
> Over the sea to Skye.

Wandering in the Highlands after his defeat at *Culloden, Bonnie Prince Charlie* was helped to hide by many loyal Scots, even though they would have welcomed the reward of £30 000 which had been put on his head.

Flora Macdonald agreed to help the prince escape from Benbecula, but while make preparations she was arrested by the militia for not having a passport. She asked to see their commanding officer, her stepfather, who ordered her release and supplied her with a passport naming herself, a manservant Neil MacEachain and Betty Burke, her servant, who would really be the prince. Thus disguised, they fled to Skye by boat. From there the prince went on to Raasay while Flora returned home. Flora Macdonald was later arrested for her part in the escape and kept in custody (in the house of a private family) in London until a general amnesty released her in 1747. In 1750 she married Alexander Macdonald of Kingsburgh and went with him to America. She died in Skye in 1790 and was buried there in a shroud which she had chosen for herself in her youth and had carried about with her all over the world.

One of the many romantic songs which is associated with the name of Bonnie Prince Charlie, 'The Skye Boat-song', relates to Flora

Macdonald's heroic rescue. People often think that it was written by a Scotsman at the time; however it was written during the 1880s by an Englishman, Harald Boulton.

(See Roderick *Mackenzie*.)

Mackenzie, Roderick When *Bonnie Prince Charlie* was wandering and hiding among the hills after the defeat at *Culloden*, this man, who bore a striking resemblance to Charles, was taken prisoner by some soldiers. Though he defended himself, it was clear that he was going to be captured and killed. Hoping to do some good for the *Jacobite* cause before he died, he called out, 'Villains, you have slain your prince.' The soldiers, thinking they had killed Charles Stuart, sent his head to London and for a time the search for Charles was called off.

Maidens, the These two mountains are to be found in the region of Lochaber, bounded by Loch Linnhe and Loch Leven.

A story relates that a famous deer hunter who lived in the area had a favourite greyhound which was getting old and slowing up. One autumn day the hunter and his dog were out after deer but the dog was too old and tired to catch any. At the end of the day the hunter sat down sadly, thinking that both his and the dog's hunting days were past. At that moment two beautiful young women appeared and gave the hunter a dog, Brodum, which they said was faster than any creature on the earth. Eager to try out the speed of his new dog, the hunter set off once more and caught a huge amount of deer. Next day the hunter gathered his family at the foot of the mountains and said, 'From this day forth these mountains shall be called the Maidens.'

Maid of Norway Margaret was living in Norway when her grandfather, Alexander III of Scotland, died. Since she was only four years old, it was decided that the country should be ruled by six nobles who were to act as regents until she was older. After a while, the nobles began to fight amongst each other, so it was thought best that she should come to Scotland. In 1290, aged eight, the 'Maid' was sent off in a ship to Scotland but on the voyage she became very ill and died. No one knows how she died or where she was buried and some people suspected at the time that she had been murdered.

The death of the Maid left the people of Scotland in great difficulties as she had been the only direct heir to the throne. A number of nobles put themselves forward as candidates for the throne, among them Robert de Brus (father of Robert *Bruce*). Eventually, in 1292, Edward I of England, the *'Hammer of the Scots'* helped to put the weak John *Baliol* on the Scottish throne to rule as a puppet for him – an act which contributed to the start of the Scottish Wars of Independence (1296–1328).

Marmalade A legend tells us that marmalade first came to Scotland with *Mary Queen of Scots.*

Not being used to the cold, wet weather when she arrived from France, Mary caught a bad cold. To cheer her up, one of her French maids concocted a mixture of stewed oranges and sugar and took a bowlful to the queen. As the smell wafted along the corridors of Holyrood Palace one of the men at arms asked what was in the bowl. Unable to speak Scots the maid replied, *'Marie est malade'* (Mary is ill) which the soldier understood as 'marmalade'.

Traditional orange marmalade certainly does bear a strong resemblance to the following recipe for *compote d'oranges* which has been translated and adapted from a sixteenth-century French cookery book.

Take 12 bitter oranges and 2 lemons. Cut the fruit in half and squeeze out the juice. Slice the fruit thinly and put in a pan with the juice, pips tied in a muslin bag and 6 pints (3.5 litres) water. Bring to the boil and simmer gently without a lid for approximately 2 hours. The liquid should be reduced by half and the peel should be very soft. Remove the pips and add 6½ pounds (3 kg) sugar, stirring until it has all dissolved. Boil rapidly for about 15 minutes. Test for setting. Leave 15 minutes before potting and covering.

Martinmas The feast of St Martin falls on 11 November, also the feast day of *St Andrew*. It is a *Quarter-day* in Scotland. On this date, because the fodder was exhausted, the beasts were slaughtered and salted or dried for the winter.

Mary Queen of Scots (1542–87) The daughter of James V and Mary of Guise is remembered as one of Scotland's most tragic figures, a beautiful woman whose heart ruled her head. Mary was only seven days old when her father died and she became queen of Scotland. Almost immediately, two parties began to fight for control of the baby queen and the country. The Roman Catholics, loyal to the queen mother, produced a document which gave their Cardinal Beaton charge of the child but when this was discovered to be a forgery, the Earl of Arran, a Protestant, was chosen to be regent.

Mary lived in Scotland until she was six when, in an attempt to put a halt to the *'Rough Wooing'*, she was sent to France, taking with her the companions whom the Scots call the *Four Maries*. Mary married the Dauphin who later became Francis II of France.

More French than Scots, it was as a stranger that she returned to her native land in 1561 – a widow at the age of nineteen.

She arrived at Leith on 19 August to cold inhospitable weather and unfriendly nobles. The Protestants refused to accept a return to Roman Catholicism and Mary had to agree that Scotland was never again to be subject to Rome. This she did on the condition that she be allowed to follow her faith, which she did in private.

In 1565 Mary married her cousin Henry, Lord

Darnley and, without any allowance from the Scots parliament, proclaimed him king of Scots. By the following year their relationship had cooled and Darnley became immensely jealous of his wife's secretary, the Italian David Rizzio. One evening in March, Darnley led a party of nobles into the room where Mary was sitting with a lady-in-waiting and Rizzio. Knowing that Darnley intended to kill him, Rizzio clung in terror to the queen's skirts and begged for mercy, but to no avail. The nobles dragged the screaming man into another room where they stabbed him, leaving him to bleed to death at the door of the queen's chamber. Mary was to give birth to James VI only three months later.

A year later Darnley himself was murdered, the victim of an explosion which blew up the house of Kirk o' Field where he lay ill. It was believed that Mary had arranged the murder in order to be free to marry James Hepburn, Earl of Bothwell, which she did in May 1567, just twelve days after he divorced his wife and three months after Darnley's death. Mary was charged with complicity in the murder, forced to abdicate, and imprisoned at Loch Leven Castle but managed to escape to England where she hoped to get help from her cousin Elizabeth I.

Elizabeth held her in custody, ostensibly waiting for proof that Mary was innocent. Proof came in the form of the 'Casket Letters', supposedly written in Mary's own hand, and which purport to show that Mary was involved in the killing. Mary insisted that the letters had been forged by her half-brother, Moray, but Elizabeth continued to keep the Scots queen imprisoned.

More letters sealed her fate when a rich English Catholic, Anthony Babington, conspired with thirteen others to murder Elizabeth and rescue Mary. Though Mary denied all knowledge of the 'Babington Conspiracy' letters were produced, again supposedly written by her. Mary was put on trial at Fotheringhay Castle on 14 October 1586, charged with conspiracy against Elizabeth, and beheaded on 8 February 1587.

May Day Also called *Beltane,* this is a festival of purely pagan origin which greets the beginning of summer. In olden times fires were lit and people danced in the woods and fields where fertility rites were carried out before the sowing of the crops. May Day is also celebrated as an international workers' holiday on which Labour rallies and marches take place.

Memorates/Memorats The name given by the Swedish folklorist Carl von Sydow for stories told as true experiences. These stories do not have the tight structure of a folk-tale and are told in a casual, conversational tone.

(See *AT Index.*)

Mistletoe *(Viscum album)* Mistletoe is a plant which was much revered by the old Celts. Called the 'Golden Bough' it played a major part in their worship. A kiss under the mistletoe at Christmas-time is said to hark back to the Norse legend which says that an arrow made of mistletoe wood was used to kill Balder, the god of light. The old gods condemned the plant for ever to have to look on while pretty girls were kissed.

N

National Anthem

> Scots, wha hae wi' Wallace bled,
> Scots, wham Bruce has aften led,
> Welcome to your gory bed,
> Or to victorie.

Written by *Burns* in 1793, 'Robert Bruce's March to Bannockburn' (commonly called 'Scots, Wha Hae') is the national anthem of Scotland. Burns wrote the words to the tune 'Hey Tuttie Tattie', reputedly played by the Scots as they marched against Edward II at Bannockburn (1314). The words were imagined by Burns as what *Bruce* said to his troops on the eve of the battle in which an estimated 8000 Scots were victorious over at least 18 000 English.

The British national anthem, 'God Save the Queen', became popular at the time of the *Forty-five* as a demonstration of loyalty towards George II. The words 'confound their politics' in the second verse refer to the *Jacobites*.

Nemo Me Impune Lacessit The Scottish motto, meaning 'no one provokes me with impunity' is rendered in Scots as 'Wha daur meddle wi' me' (Who dares to interfere with me). It is also the motto of the *Knights of the Thistle*.

Numbers A lot of *superstitions* are associated with numbers. Odd numbers are generally thought to be lucky, even numbers unlucky. A person born on the first day of the month is particularly fortunate whereas someone born on the second is very unlucky. The Greek god Pluto, who was assigned the second month of the year, was thought to be evil.

Three is a lucky number and three times three even luckier. However, working on the principle that 'everything goes in threes' it is widely believed that when two people die a third will follow.

Seven, being a mystical or sacred number, is extremely good. A seventh child is very lucky and the seventh son of a seventh son is thought to have the ability to cure and to have *second sight.* A birth date which is divisible by seven ensures good fortune for life.

Thirteen is considered unlucky not only in Scotland. The number is associated both with the Last Supper where Christ and his twelve disciples made up thirteen and with the Norse god Loki, the spirit of evil and strife, who was a troublesome thirteenth guest at a banquet in Valhalla. The Scots call any Friday which falls on the thirteenth of the month 'Black Friday'.

O

Old Pretender James Francis Edward Stuart (1688–1766), was the father of *Bonnie Prince Charlie* (the 'Young Pretender'). The 1707 Treaty of Union between Scotland and England forced the Scots to accept a Hanoverian succession to the throne, but many Scots regarded the only son of the deposed James VII and II as Scotland's rightful king. The 'Old Pretender', as the Hanoverians called him, made three attempts to regain the throne in 1708, 1715 (the *Fifteen*) and 1719. All failed and he died in exile in Rome on 1 January 1766.

Onion Long known in Scotland as a cure for a cold. It can either be boiled and the water drunk, or eaten raw. Hot onion skins as a poultice are good for a sore throat.

Oral Tradition Folklorists use this term to mean poetry, stories, rhymes, sayings and songs handed down over the centuries by word of mouth.

Before the invention of printing in the fifteenth century only a privileged few were literate so most stories were communicated independently of manuscript or print. Mother passed on nursery rhymes and songs to child, father and son shared jokes and riddles, and the *bard* recited epic poems and heroic ballads telling the history of the *clan*. Weather- and *plant-lore* was common knowledge in agricultural communities and the goings-on of the elite were known to the masses through ballads and tales.

Oral communication is a fluid and versatile medium. Words change through mishearing or misunderstanding and deliberate changes are often made in order to give a story or song an immediate flavour. Many political jokes which are to be heard today have been kept alive for centuries by changing the name of the politician or party concerned. Though the oral tradition has all but died out in many countries, Scotland is fortunate in that there are still singers and story-tellers among the people who have learned their repertoire by word of mouth from parents or grandparents.

(See *School of Scottish Studies.*)

P

Picts From the Latin *pictus* meaning 'painted'. These ancient Scots, first mentioned in Roman chronicles in 296 AD, lived mainly in north-eastern Scotland. As no traces of their language remain, no one knows where they originated, though some recent research suggests that they may have used a Brittonic dialect and may therefore have been related to the Welsh, Cornish and Breton peoples.

The Picts disappeared very suddenly from the history of Scotland around the middle of the ninth century. At this time Kenneth MacAlpin claimed the Pictish crown – his mother had been a Pictish princess – and successfully subdued the Picts into accepting him as their king.

The story goes that MacAlpin invited all the Scots nobles to a feast to try to persuade them to fight for him. The nobles were unwilling but in the night MacAlpin sent his servants dressed as ghosts to the bedsides of his guests to encourage them to fight. Next day they appeared for battle. The Picts asked the Saxons for help but they ran away, leaving the Pictish army in disarray to be slaughtered by MacAlpin. The Pictish lands were given to Scots nobles who gave them Scottish names and so the memory of the Picts vanished.

In Scottish folklore they are often thought of as a race of dwarfs who lived underground and ancient barrows (burial mounds) are often attributed to them. Some *travelling people* say that they are descendants of the Picts as both peoples are noted tinsmiths.

Plant-lore Plants figure very often in folklore stories and proverbs. Certain trees, like the *elder* and the *rowan* provide protection against *witches* and folk-medicine uses plants containing a chemical or oil which is known to cure illness or disease. Folk-names for plants can tell us what their properties are – 'eye-bright' (*Euphrasia rostkoviana*) for eye complaints and 'piss-a-bed' (*dandelion*), containing an alkaloid which has diuretic properties, for kidney and bladder troubles.

Prince's Strand This was the name given to the small sandy cove where *Bonnie Prince Charlie* first set foot on British soil. On the island of Eriskay, between Barra and South Uist, the cove boasts some beautiful pink convolvulus plants which are said to have grown from some seeds which Charles had in his pocket when he left France.

Despite the beauty of the plants, the cove is thought to have something evil about it, for the small house which stands there, in which Charles and his companions are thought to have spent their first night in Scotland, is said to be haunted.

Q

Quarter-days Following the old Celtic calendar, the Scottish year is divided into four at *Candlemas* (2 February); *Whitsun* (15 May); *Lammas* (1 August) and *Martinmas* (11 November). Still used today as legal term days, when rent has to be paid or the tenancy of a house begins or ends, they were also the days when servants and farm workers were hired.

(See *Fairs.*)

R

Red-Caps Living in castles or towers in Lowland Scotland, these are the nastiest of the Scottish *fairies,* who kill their victims by rolling boulders on to them before collecting the blood in their caps for drinking. Crucifixes and quotations from the Bible are the only things which red-caps are afraid of.

Red Fox The name for Colin Campbell of Glenure, murdered in 1752. Despite speculation over the last centuries, no one really knows to this day who committed the so-called *Appin murder.*

Resurrectionists A name for body-snatchers, the people who dug up newly buried bodies in the nineteenth century to supply anatomists with specimens to dissect. With sacking over the horse's hoofs to muffle the noise, the resurrectionists would drive their coaches round the churchyards at dead of night looking for newly dug graves from which to remove bodies. Resurrectionists were so prevalent that some families kept vigil in the graveyard at night while others put iron railings over the graves of their loved-ones to keep their bodies safe. Grave railings can still be seen in some Scottish churchyards today.

The best known body-snatchers, *Burke and Hare,* were not resurrectionists in the true sense. Rather than going out at night to cold cemeteries they murdered their victims in the comfort of Hare's flat in Edinburgh's Tanner's Close. Unlike the bodies which the other resurrectionists delivered, the doctors at the School of Anatomy were always sure of getting a fresh corpse from them.

Riddles 'What goes up when the rain comes down?' Answer: An umbrella.

A riddle is a short composition in which some thing or creature is described in an obscure way or with a neat turn of phrase. They can also use a play on words or pun.

Riddles are an ancient art, going back to Roman times. Popular in Britain from at least the eighth century, riddles often have their foreign equivalents.

Robertson, Jeannie (1908–75) The great Aberdeen ballad singer Jeannie Robertson was 'discovered' by fieldworkers at the *School of Scottish Studies* in 1953. A marvellous interpreter of the *Child Ballads* as well as a good songwriter, Jeannie Robertson came from a family of *travelling people* and was also a renowned story-teller. Her daughter, Lizzie Higgins, carries on the tradition.

Robin Redbreast According to tradition, the robin pricked its breast when it tried to pull the thorns from Christ's head when He was on the cross. The robin started to bleed and has had a red breast ever since. It is thought to be very unlucky to kill or cage a robin and taking eggs from a robin's nest will bring certain misfortune.

(See *Holly.*)

Rob Roy Robert MacGregor (1671–1734), also known as 'Robert the Red' because of his red hair. A favourite with youngsters, who imagine him as a

type of Robin Hood character, Rob Roy was a *Jacobite* outlaw, freebooter and sheep-stealer. A lot of his fame is due to the recounting of his adventures in *Scott*'s *Rob Roy* (published in 1818), where he is described as being smaller than average though strong and agile with broad shoulders, giving him '. . . something the air of being too square . . .'

Rough Wooing, the When James V died his daughter, *Mary Queen of Scots,* was only seven days old.

Henry VIII of England took the opportunity of the Scots' disarray to try to unite his country with Scotland by proposing the marriage of his son, Edward, to the baby Mary. The regent, the Earl of Arran, agreed that when Mary was old enough the wedding would take place.

Henry wanted Mary to be brought up at the English court but the Scots refused and finally called the marriage off.

In response, Henry gathered an army and ships and set off for Scotland, arriving in Edinburgh in May 1544 to commence the 'Rough Wooing' – the use of force to persuade the Scots to agree to the marriage. His army retreated, unsuccessful. After Henry VIII's death in 1547 the English renewed their attacks, defeating the Scots at the Battle of Pinkie (1547). Even so, the Scots refused to agree to the marriage. Mary was sent to France the following year, where she remained at court until 1561. The Treaty of Boulogne in 1549 at last brought the war and the Rough Wooing to an end.

Rowan Tree (Sorbus aucuparia) Scots believe that a rowan branch hung over the door of a house or a barn will keep *witches* and evil spirits away.

Davie Ritchie, a badly deformed man, was well known in the Borders in the early nineteenth century for his knowledge of plants and the *superstitions* connected with them. Just before he died Davie asked for a rowan to be planted near his grave to keep him safe from witches. This was duly done, but the tree was not enough to frighten off the *resurrectionists* who knew that Davie's unusual physique would bring an extra good price from the anatomists.

Rue (Ruta graveolens) This plant, which soothes and heals, is supposed to cure people who have been poisoned. Symbolically it is associated with repentance and regret, compunction and compassion. It was the emblem of the *Picts*.

S

St Andrew Together with *Columba,* St Andrew is the partron saint of Scotland. Some people believe that St Andrew's remains were brought to Scotland in the fourth century, while others say that in AD 731 St Andrew's relics were brought to the Fife town which now bears his name. A monastery which had been founded by an assistant of *Columba* had been situated there since the end of the sixth century.

St Andrew's Day (11 November) is celebrated with a party or a *ceilidh* by Scots all over the world.

St Andrew's Cross Folklore offers two versions of how this X-shaped cross was chosen as the standard for the Scots. Those who believe that the remains of *St Andrew* were brought to Scotland in the fourth century say that the *crux decussata* on which Andrew was martyred was adopted at that time. Others, who date the arrival of St Andrew's remains as the eighth century, claim that the cross appeared in the sky the night before Hungus, King

of the *Picts* from AD 731 to 761, defeated the Saxons in a battle. Those who favour the latter version say that the dark blue background to the white cross represents the night sky.

St Andrew's Day St Andrew's Day (11 November), used to be celebrated all over Scotland. At the time of the Reformation the tradition stopped with the result that the day often passes unnoticed in Scotland. Expatriot Scots, however, do celebrate with a dance and a meal, usually organized by St Andrew Societies, foreign friendly societies founded abroad in the nineteenth century to help emigrant Scots. A St Andrew's Day celebration follows a similar form to a *Burns Supper* but the poetry recitations are often replaced by speeches.

St Kentigern St Kentigern, also known as St Mungo, from 'Mungho' meaning 'dearest', lived some time around the beginning of the seventh century. He is known as the traditional founder of Glasgow Cathedral and is patron saint of the city. His symbols, a cross, a salmon and a ring, allude to a popular legend about him.

The queen of Cadzow had been untrue to her husband, King Roderick, and had given her lover her ring. When the king found out about it, he stole the ring, threw it into the river Clyde and then asked the queen for it. The queen went to St Kentigern to beg for help and he, after praying to the cross, went to the river and caught a salmon which carried the ring in its mouth. He gave the ring to the queen and restored harmony to the couple and the people.

Glasgow's coat of arms include the salmon with the ring in its mouth.

(See *Tree That Never Grew*.)

Sandy Bell's Bar

> My mother's name was Annie,
> My father's name was Dan.
> Come sit beside me, come hear my sad tale,
> I've been wronged by a Sandy Bell's man.

Edinburgh's Forest Hill Bar, to give it its proper name, has been the meeting place of folk-singers from the time of the start of the folk revival in the early fifties. Especially on a Saturday afternoon singers, who were later to become famous names on the folk scene, used to meet for a session of guitar-playing, fiddling, singing and, of course, drinking. 'Bell's' was renovated in the eighties, decorated with etched mirrors, and has now lost much of its style. Many of the old regulars now go elsewhere, though 'sessions' still take place on a Sunday. Some of the Edinburgh characters who used to meet there have been epitomized in the novel *The Myrtle and the Ivy* by the late Stuart MacGregor, writer of the folk-song 'Sandy Bell's Man'. The name 'Sandy Bell' refers to the son of one of the earlier landladies of the pub.

School of Scottish Studies Founded in 1951 as a research and fieldwork establishment, the school is Scotland's national archive of *oral tradition* containing a vast collection of songs, stories, music and information about traditional ways of life in Scotland.

In a proposal placed before the Senate of the University of Edinburgh on 10 May 1950, the following extensive list of activities were proposed for the School:

A   Archaeology;
B   A compilation of information upon which maps of prehistoric and historic Scotland could be based;
C   The collection of place names from both documentary and oral sources and the organization of a place name archive;
D   The collection of oral traditions of all parts of Scotland and the organization of an equivalent folklore archive for these;
E   Study of the structure of the European and other affinities of music in Scotland;
F   The integration of intensified field studies in social anthropology with the rest of the work of the School;

G The co-ordination of the study of Scots Law in relation to the other studies in the School.

The Senate gave the project their approval and, with the aid of the Carnegie Trust, the School of Scottish Studies was founded. Its offices are situated in two houses which also accommodate the offices of the Linguistic Survey of Scotland and those of the two national dictionaries, the Scottish National and the Dictionary of the Older Scottish Tongue.

As a result of the collection and investigation done to date, the archive of the School contains a vast wealth of material of all kinds. Amongst these are thousands of stories and songs – handwritten in the early days, nowadays collected and preserved on tape.

Since 1969 the School has functioned as a department of Edinburgh University's Faculty of Arts. Not only for academics, it is the place where Scotland's folk-singers go to look for new material or to find out more about songs they are interested in.

Scotia One of the names for Scotland.

Legend has it that a Greek prince called Gathelus married an Egyptian princess called Scota whom he loved so much that he decreed that his people should be called Scots in her honour. At the time of the plagues of Egypt, Gathelus and Scota left Egypt and sailed to Spain, where they lived for some years.

After living there in peace for some time they were driven out of the country by the Spaniards and two sons of Gathelus and Scota, Hiberus and Minecus, set sail to find another place for them to settle in. The place they found was Ireland which is sometimes called Hibernia in honour of Hiberus.

So the Scots settled in Ireland where they taught the people how to plough and sow. Many generations of kings of Ireland were descended from them and one of them, a prince called Rothesay, sailed off to the east and landed on the island which is now called Bute, (and its main town

Rothesay). Finding that the island was fertile and good for breeding cattle, Rothesay brought more and more Scots over from Hibernia, who eventually infiltrated the north-western part of Scotland. In early medieval Latin the word *Scotus* signified an Irishman, Ireland was known as Scotia Major, and Scotland Scotia Minor.

Scott, Sir Walter (1771–1832) Sir Walter Scott was the first *antiquary* to use folklore to good effect in works of literature, weaving romances laced with the tales and adventures that he heard from old women, old *Jacobite* warriors, peasants and fishermen.

Scott's love of folklore is to be seen in all his works, which are packed with quotations from *ballads,* traditional songs and poems, *superstitions* and country-lore. In detailed prefaces and notes concerning primary sources Scott gives due respect to the people from whom he heard the stories which gave him the ideas for his novels. *Waverley* contains tales told to Scott as a child and the plot for *Guy Mannering,* which was completed in just six weeks, originated in a tale told to him by an old servant of his father's.

His first major work of non-fiction, the three-volume *Minstrelsy of the Scottish Border* (1802–3), was a collection of ballads gathered in southern Scotland to which he added essays about local history, superstitions and legends.

Scottish Country Dancing What is known today as Scottish country dancing is a mixture of ancient native dances and foreign dances which have been added to them and influenced them over the centuries.

Elements still remain today of ritual dances performed by the earliest inhabitants of Scotland to ensure fertility or a good hunt. Many circle dances may hark back to the worship of pagan gods where the movement of the circle is usually clockwise, in the direction of the sun, for good luck. Bridal reels, either foursomes, performed by the bride and groom with the bridesmaid and best man, or sixsomes to include an older married couple, are the remains of old fertility rites, danced to ensure a happy and fruitful marriage. Together with these native peasant dances go foreign court dances, some of which may have been brought to Scotland as early as the eleventh century.

Controversy abounds as to why 'country' dance is so called. Some historians suggest that it comes from the word *contrapassi,* a sort of figure dance mentioned in books of Italian dancing masters; some say it comes from the French *contre* meaning 'opposite' because couples dance opposite each other, whereas others say that the French took the English word 'country' and changed it to *contre.* Yet another theory is that these dances were first performed at court masques and danced in a country setting as a sort of pastoral dance.

Perhaps what helped to fix country dancing so firmly among other Scottish traditions was the visit of George IV organized by Sir Walter *Scott* in 1822. Filling Edinburgh with Highland chiefs, kilts, tartanalia and other manifestations of fake-lore, the visit was a round of banquets and balls in which Scottish dancing was performed with zeal. George threw himself wholeheartedly into the whole thing, going so far as to don the *kilt.* As one Edinburgh matron put it when she saw his fat figure swathed in *tartan:* 'With his stay being so short, the more we see of him the better.'

The Royal Scottish Country Dance Society, formed as the Scottish Country Dance Society in Glasgow in 1923 to preserve what was thought to be a dying tradition, now has over 28 000 members all over the world. As well as documenting dances and training teachers, the RSCDS organizes dances in Scotland and abroad.

Apart from these formal gatherings, informal dances and *ceilidhs* take place regularly wherever a few Scots meet and most especially on *Burns's* birthday and *St Andrew's* night.

Sea Cattle and Sea Serpents On the island of Wester Ross they say that cattle which yield good milk have been served by a sea bull. People often claim to have seen a strange bull amongst the cattle when the milk yield is particularly good.

A sea serpent or a snake which had grown to an enormous size has also sometimes been seen in that area. Fishermen used to protect themselves against it with a *charm* in the form of an amulet or a rhyme.

Some people think that the *Loch Ness Monster* is a sea serpent.

Seannachie A hereditary genealogist and story-teller of a *clan*.

One famous seannachie story tells of the clan MacDonald, tracing the origins of the family to a seal woman or *silkie*, the daughter of the king of the seals.

Her name was Fionna, the 'fair one' and she lived in the Western Isles. MacDonald was young and very handsome and his people wanted him to marry, but he could not find anyone to love among the girls he knew. He decided the best thing to do was to put all the names of the eligible young women into a hat, draw out one name at random and marry her. With this thought in mind he went out for a sail in his boat. Not paying any attention to where he was going, he was surprised to hear a voice saying, 'If you do not turn your boat she will break on the rocks.'

MacDonald looked up and saw the most beautiful young woman and fell in love with her immediately. 'Who are you?' he asked.

'I'm the daughter of the king of the seals,' she said.

'Will you marry me?' asked the Lord of the Isles.

Fionna smiled as she replied, 'I can't do that without my father's permission and he's not here at the moment . . . but he'll be back in a week.'

A week later MacDonald returned to the same place and asked for the hand of the seal king's daughter. The seal king agreed, but only on the condition that MacDonald should bring clothes for her. 'She will leave me with nothing,' said the king.

'And with nothing I will take her,' said Mac-Donald, promising to return one month later.

When he came back he brought fine clothes and a beautiful golden coronet set with pearls – but he forgot to bring shoes. When MacDonald and his bride were ready to go the king turned to his daughter and said, 'Promise me this: if ever an unkind word should pass the lips of your husband you must return immediately to me.'

'I promise,' said Fionna. And off she went with her husband to his home.

At first the couple were very happy and after a while they had a son but, very slowly, things started to change between them. Fionna had to stay with the child while MacDonald went away on business and one evening he stayed overlong at a party on the mainland. When he came back and found her gazing sadly at the sea, he was angry with himself for having left her alone, but instead of saying that he was sorry, he said nothing. The baby was crying and MacDonald said angrily, 'Can you not make the child quiet.' At this Fionna looked at him sadly, lifted the baby and kissed it and put it back in his cot. She then went out of the room and down to the shore where she stripped off her clothes and dived into the sea to return to her father.

MacDonald was a sad and sorry man. He lay in his room grieving and some people thought he would die, but after seven days he came out and got on with his life again for he had to look after the child. But when the boy was twenty-one, MacDonald gave him the keys to the castle, got into his boat and sailed away towards the Western Isles, never to be seen again. Some people believe that he made it up with his wife whose father gave him the power to change himself into a seal.

Second Sight The ability to see into the future. The 'seer' does not 'call up' apparitions like a spiritualist or a medium, but sees what is going to happen in the future in visions which come at any place, at any time, of their own volition.

The gift is not peculiar to Scotland, but there are more records of seers than in other countries.

Though some highly intelligent people have been recorded as having second sight, it is not restricted to people of great intelligence or high birth. In fact, more often than not, the person who is reputed to have the 'sight' is an ordinary man or woman. Coinneach Odhar, the *Brahan Seer*, who foresaw the construction of the Caledonian Canal almost 250 years before it was built, was a farm labourer.

The gift of second sight can be inherited and is often passed on from a seventh son to a seventh son. It can also be passed on temporarily by the seer placing his hand on another's head and a foot on the other's foot. People believe that *Thomas the Rhymer*, who lived in the thirteenth century, was given his visionary power by the *elf* queen.

(See *Fortune Telling*.)

Seven Men of Glenmoriston When *Bonnie Prince Charlie* was hiding in the hills after the defeat at *Culloden* he was befriended and helped by these seven outlaws. The men, who had fought for the *Jacobite* cause, were afraid to return to their homes. They were living wild attacking the soldiers of *'Bloody Butcher'* Cumberland.

When Charles came upon the seven men, he was afraid to tell them who he was for he thought that they would hand him over to the authorities for the £30 000 reward which was on his head. He passed himself off as the son of a Highland chieftain, but the men recognized him. Far from turning him over to the troops, however, even though it would have gained them not only the reward, but a pardon, the men helped him. It is said that one of them even went into the nearest town in disguise to hear the news and keep Charles informed of how things were going in the search for him. In the course of their marches with the prince an eighth man joined the band and took their oath to fight against Cumberland and his army until the day of their deaths.

Seven Men of Moidart The seven men who sailed for Scotland with *Bonnie Prince Charlie* from Nantes in summer, 1745.

The men were Aeneas MacDonald, a banker in Paris and friend of the prince; Sir Thomas Sheridan, Charles's seventy-year-old Irish tutor; the Reverend George Kelly, an English clergyman; John O'Sullivan, an Irish officer in the French service; Sir John MacDonald, a lieutenant-colonel of the Irish cavalry brigade who was in the Spanish service; Colonel Francis Strickland, an Englishman; and, perhaps the most important member of the party, Duke William of Atholl, called Lord Tullibardine as he had been deprived of his title because of his *Jacobite* leanings.

On 5 July 1745 the prince with his companions and retinue set sail in two ships, the *Du Teillay* (or *Doutelle*) and the *Elizabeth*. The latter was attacked by an English ship, the *Lion,* just off the Lizard in Cornwall. After a battle lasting five hours, the *Lion* gave up the fight, leaving the *Elizabeth* so badly damaged that all she could do was to return to Brest with her wounded and dead. Charles continued with his friends in the *Du Teillay* and arrived on Eriskay in the Western Isles, landing on *Prince's Strand* on 23 July.

Silkie The silkies live near the Shetland Islands where they take the form of seals with very glittering eyes. On nights when there is a full moon they come on land, take off their seal skins and dance. If a human should steal their skin, the silkie will follow them and ask for it back. If a female silkie loses her skin, she is often willing to marry the man who has stolen it but, though silkies make good housewives and mothers, they always long to return to the sea. Legend says that they can only do this if they get hold of their seal skins again, but the *seannachie* story of the *clan* MacDonald makes no mention of the skin of the silkie wife who returned to her own people after being hurt by her husband.

Silkies who are in the form of human women can be recognized by the webbed skin between their fingers, their rough palms and slow breathing. They are also good swimmers.

Spunkie A good spirit, it gets its name from the Scots word *spunk* – a small fire, which refers to the little lights that they carry. Like their English relatives, the 'will-o'-the-wisp', spunkies are thought to be the souls of children who have died before *baptism*. The hollows they haunt are called spunkie-howes.

Stevenson, Robert Louis Scottish author, born Edinburgh, 13 November 1850, died Samoa, 1894. As a child Stevenson was often ill and confined to bed. To keep him amused his nurse, Cummie, told him folk-tales which he called 'Tales from the Land of Counterpane'. Many elements from these tales were used in his novels by Stevenson, who also drew on real-life events from Scottish history. *Kidnapped* (published in 1886) and *Catriona* (1893) are *Jacobite* romances, the former including a description of the murder of the *Red Fox*.

When Robert Louis Stevenson was forty-one he gave away his birthday by deed of gift to a young friend, Annie Ide, who had been born '. . . out of all reason' on Christmas Day, saying that, at forty-one, he no longer had need of birthdays. Every year after receiving the gift Annie celebrated her birthday on 13 November, reading the Deed of Gift aloud at a party. When she died she left the unusual birthday present to one of her nieces.

Stone of Destiny

> Now the Dean o' Westminster was a powerful man,
> He held a' the reins o' the State in his hand.
> But for a' his great power it flustered him nane,
> Till some rogues ran away wi' his wee magic stane.

> *o'* – of;   *a'* – all;   *nane* – none;   *wee* – little;
> *stane* – stone

The Stone of Destiny, Stone of Scone or *Lia-fàil,* is a four-hundredweight block of red sandstone, thought to have been brought to the Scots-Irish kingdom of *Dalriada* at the start of the sixth century. The stone, which is supposed to have great magic powers, is also called the Coronation Stone and, in times past, kings of Scotland were crowned on it.

In 1296 the Stone was removed from Scone, the traditional seat of government, by Edward I *'Hammer of the Scots'* and placed in Westminster Abbey, where it remained until 26 December 1950. On that date it was reclaimed for Scotland by four students, who drove to London and lifted the Stone from underneath the Coronation Chair, took it to Arbroath, the place where the *Declaration of Arbroath* (Scotland's declaration of independence) had been signed in 1320, and left it at the high altar of the ruined abbey.

Meanwhile, in London, newspaper headlines screamed 'Act of sacrilege', 'Student rag' and 'Senseless crime!' Their act, however, was a serious attempt to return a piece of stolen property to the people of Scotland.

When the Stone was eventually recovered and removed once more to Westminster a number of jokes, stories and folk-songs about the incident started. The end of all of these is that the stone in Westminster is a copy and that the real Stone is still in Scotland.

Superstition Defined in *Chambers English Dictionary* as 'ignorant and irrational belief in supernatural agency, omens, divination, sorcery etc'. Superstitions, with their roots in religion and folklore, are known by everyone all over the world. Scotland is particularly rich in superstitions, some of which it shares with other countries – the unlucky number thirteen being probably the most widespread superstition in Christian countries because there were thirteen guests at the Last Supper.

Some superstitions only to be found in Scotland are: crossing **knives**, which could result in a quarrel. The superstition derives from the old times when people crossed swords in a fight.

A **spade** mistakenly taken indoors is a *death* omen. Probably because it has to do with grave-diggers.

Because it is such a special time for the Scots there are many superstitions concerning New Year and *Hogmanay: first-footing,* in which a visitor brings certain traditionally lucky gifts into the house, the custom of cleaning the house thoroughly on New Year's Eve and, most important, *never* to sweep up on 1 January. This brings misfortune to the house and its occupants for the whole of the coming year.

(See *Charm, Luck, Numbers.*)

Sylvander *Burns* first called himself by this name in a letter dated 28 December 1787. The recipient, Mrs Agnes McLehose, he called *Clarinda,* saying, 'I like the idea of Arcadian names.'

T

Jock Tamson The Scots everyman or Adam. A common phrase in Scotland is 'We're all Jock Tamson's Bairns,' meaning, 'Everyone is equal.'

Tartan The material used for the early *kilt* was woven in various coloured checks and stripes. The material was called plaiden, the blanket-like cloth a plaid. Because the dyes for the colours came from local plants, people from different areas wore differently coloured plaids. When the cult of the kilt was taken up by the upper classes following the visit of George IV to Edinburgh in 1822 many tartans were invented to represent the colours of various *clans.* Nowadays visitors to Scotland can find out about 'their' clan tartan by computer and can buy virtually anything in the pattern.

Thistle

> Hurrah for the Thistle!
> The brave Scottish thistle,
> The evergreen thistle of Scotland for me!

The thistle played an important part in the early history of Scotland. It is said that in the tenth century, when Danes tried to invade the country, creeping stealthily at night, one of them stood on a thistle and screamed in pain. The Scots were then alerted and the invasion was prevented. King Kenneth III immediately adopted the thistle as the Scots national emblem.

Thomas the Rhymer *Child Ballad* No 37

> Oh True Thomas he lay
> On the Huntly bank,
> Beneath an eildon tree;
> Oh when he saw a lady fair
> Coming riding ower the lea.

Thomas Rymour of Erceldoune, known as Thomas the Rhymer or True Thomas, lived in the thirteenth century, and has had a reputation as a prophet since that time. One of his predictions is recorded in a manuscript written before 1320 and he is referred to in a French chronicle written in 1355.

His prophetic power was given to him by the *elf* queen who took him on horseback to her country where he remained for seven years. On his return to the world, the queen gave Thomas the gift of soothsaying but made him swear that he would go back to her if she should ever summon him. After Thomas had spent some time in his village, a neighbour came running to tell him that a white stag and a white hind were walking through the village. Thomas said, 'They have come for me,' and went to them. Later, people spoke of seeing three white deer walking over the hill and out of the village. The queen of the elves had sent for Thomas.

Travelling People The traditional tale bearers and *ballad* singers of Scotland. Rediscovered by folklorists at the *School of Scottish Studies,* these keepers of the *oral tradition* are well known at *folk festivals* and seminars at home and abroad. Families such as the Stewarts of Blairgowrie, the late Jeannie *Robertson* and her daughter Lizzie Higgins, as well as a host of others, have been recorded by commercial record companies, and traditional story-tellers such as Duncan Williamson and Stanley Robertson are enjoying some success in print at the moment.

Tree That Never Grew, the

> The tree that never grew,
> The bird that never flew,
> The fish that never swam
> The bell that never rang.

The heraldic motifs of Glasgow are a fish swimming underneath a tree which has a bell hanging on one of its branches and a bird sitting on the top.

The tree and the bell allude to the story of how *St Kentigern* hung a bell on an oak to summon the wild Scottish natives to worship. The bell, which had originally come from Rome, was used as the town's death bell until the time of the Reformation. The bird is said to be the pet *robin* which belonged to St Serf of Culross in Fife. When the bird was accidentally killed, St Kentigern brought it back to life. The fish, a salmon, is said to have carried a ring which the Queen of Cadzow gave to her lover. St Kentigern retrieved the ring and saved the royal lady from an unhappy fate.

Trows Supernatural beings which live mostly on the Shetland Islands or on Orkney. They are also called drows or sith.

Descendants of the Irish Sídhe and Scandinavian trolls, the trows lived happily together with the *Picts* in the old days and were called 'the people of peace'. In modern times, however, because of the lack of respect shown to them, they have become less friendly and have been known to steal children and cows.

U

Unicorn

> Like as a lion whose imperial power
> A proud rebellious unicorn defies.
>
> Spenser

A mythical animal with the legs of a buck, the tail of a lion and the head and body of a horse. The unicorn has a single horn in the middle of its head. Many popular beliefs surround the unicorn, among them being that a unicorn can tell if a liquid is poisoned by dipping its horn into it. Another is that a unicorn can only be captured by a virgin.

Two unicorns support the royal arms of Scotland. When James VI ascended to the throne of England he took one of the Scottish unicorns to support the royal shield, ousting the red dragon of Wales. The other armorial creature on the English shield is the *lion* and many poets and songwriters use the enmity between the lion and unicorn to portray discord between England and Scotland.

Union Jack The patron saint of Scotland is *St Andrew* and the flag of Scotland is a white *St Andrew's Cross* on a blue background. At the time of the Union of the Crowns in 1603 the English flag, a red St George's Cross on a white background, was placed on top of the Scottish flag, making the 'Union Flag'. About 100 years later, the Irish St Patrick's cross, a red X-shaped cross on a white background, was added to make the Union Jack as we know it today. The name 'Jack' comes from James VI who signed his name in French – Jacques – so his two flags came to be known as Jacks.

W

Wallace, Sir William Scotland was without a king in
1290–2 and 1296–1306 so Edward I, the *'Hammer of
the Scots',* tried very hard to force himself on the
country. One of the leaders who resisted Edward
and one of Scotland's best-loved heroes was
William Wallace.

Wallace was much taller than most men and was
supposed to have been very strong and handsome
with brown wavy hair and bright, clear eyes. Like
many heroic figures, he was also said to have been
very kind and generous and was accredited with
feats of strength which in all likelihood were
exaggerated.

One story goes that Wallace had his first fight
with the English when he was just a boy. Going
home after a day's fishing, young William met
some Englishmen. 'What have you got in that
basket?' asked one of them.

'Fish,' was the reply.

'Where did you get them?' asked another.

'I caught them in the river,' said the boy.

'Well, just you give them to me,' said the first
Englishman, 'A beggarly Scot has no need for fish.'

But William would not give up his fish and the
Englishman drew his sword. Now the boy only had
his fishing rod with him, but he was so strong that
when he hit the Englishman over the head with it
the blow killed him. Seizing the dead man's
sword, the youngster chased the other
Englishmen away.

When the English governor heard what the
young Scotsman had done he sent soldiers to take
him prisoner. But friends warned Wallace what
was going on and he escaped to the mountains to
wait until things had calmed down. It was after this
incident, according to legend, that Wallace deci-

ded to spend the rest of his life fighting the English.

Warlock Generally, the word 'warlock' (from Old English *wærloga* – traitor or devil) denotes a male *witch*, but in Scotland it is also taken to mean a black magician or someone who practises demonology.

If we believe the reports of the witch trials, devil-worship was quite common in Scotland a few centuries ago. Strangely enough, however, one of Scotland's most famous warlocks was never actually convicted of that crime.

In 1645 Major Thomas Weir became a captain in the Edinburgh City Guard. He was a *Covenanter* who lived in the West Bow with some religious zealots who called themselves the 'Bowhead Saints'. Weir was well liked and respected by the Bowhead Saints and often led the prayer meetings held in their private houses. He was an impressive-looking character, tall and dark, who seems to have enjoyed creating an air of mystery about himself by wearing a dark cloak and carrying a stick covered with carvings of the heads of strange creatures.

After twenty-five years in the West Bow it was revealed that the pious Major Weir was not all that he seemed. One evening when the Bowhead Saints had gathered, the major is said to have confessed to having an incestuous relationship with his sister, Jean. And that was not all, for he also listed a catalogue of other perversions, including bestiality. The Bowhead Saints decided Weir must be mentally ill and tried to keep him prisoner in his own house. They were afraid that people would find out about their sect so they spread a rumour that the major was dangerously ill. It seemed as if their plan would work, until the Reverend John Sinclair, minister at Ormiston, heard the story and reported it to the Lord Provost. Weir was examined by doctors who declared him sane and he and his sister were imprisoned in the Tolbooth, where Jean Weir confessed to having made a pact with the *Devil* and driving to Musselburgh in a flaming coach to meet him.

115

As proof she showed the prison guards a horseshoe-shaped mark on her forehead which she insisted had been put there by her master. She also told them that the major's stick was a magic wand which enabled him to hold sway over the Bowhead Saints and open the door to hell.

On 9 April 1670 Weir and his sister appeared in court and were charged with witchcraft. Surprisingly, they were acquitted, though sentenced to death for debauchery. Weir was hanged at the Gallow Lee, near the top of Edinburgh's Leith Walk and his sister was hanged in the Grassmarket. For some time afterwards, the house where they had lived in at the West Bow was thought to be haunted and so was boarded up.

Warts To get rid of warts rub them with a piece of bacon and bury it. When the bacon has rotted away the warts will be gone. It is important that you do not tell anyone where you have buried the bacon. Another way to get rid of warts is to spit on them and rub the spittle in. Perhaps the best-known treatment for warts is to rub them with the bark or leaves of the *elder* tree, which contains ethereal oils to kill the virus which causes warts.

Water of Life Many Scots believe that a daily 'nip' of whisky ensures a long life and many centenarians, when asked why they think they have lived so long, reply with the words 'water of life'.

Uisgebeatha (pronounced ush-ge-ba), the Gaelic word for whisky, translates as 'water of life'. The same name has been given to other types of distilled spirit: Latin – *aqua vitae*; French – *eau-de-vie*; Scandinavian – *akvavit* and Finnish – *akvaviitee*.

(See *Atholl Brose*.)

Waulking Songs These Gaelic work songs, with refrains and a chorus interspersed with solo lines, were sung while hand waulking (shrinking or fulling) tweed after it had been woven. The tweed was soaked – sometimes in soapy water, sometimes in stale urine – before being pounded by several pairs of hands to make it shrink, tightening the weave and making it water- and wind-proof.

Weatherlore The many rhymes and sayings related to the weather stem mainly from Scotland's argricultural and fishing communities. The universally known proverb – a red sky at night is a shepherd's delight, a red sky in the morning is a shepherd's warning – has its local variations throughout Scotland. One such, from the Borders, says:

If the evening is red and the morning is grey,
Then that is the sign of a bonnie new day.
If the evening is grey and the morning is red,
The lamb and the ewe will go wet to their bed.

The fisher folk in Fife know that 'When Falkland Hill puts on a cap, the Howe o' Fife will get a drap.'

drap – drop (of rain)

Weddings

Busk and go, busk and go,
Busk and go tae Cuttie's waddin'!
Wha's the lassie and the lad
Wadna gang if they were bidden?

(Dress up and go to Cuttie's wedding! Which boy and girl wouldn't go if they were invited?)

Everybody loves a traditional wedding, with the bride dressed in white to symbolize her virginity and the cake cut in imitation of its loss.

At about lunchtime on the day before her wedding, a bride is often 'creeled' by her workmates. The word 'creel' may mean 'madness' and there certainly is an air of craziness involved in this tradition which consists of decorating the bride with balloons, streamers and an 'L-plate' (the sign of an inexperienced driver) and presenting her with wooden spoons and other kitchen utensils as well as a chamber pot. The pot is filled with salt, coal and coins and the bride has to jump over it for *luck*. Travelling home in her costume, sometimes

117

pushed in a wheelbarrow by her friends, the bride is always treated to amused smiles and jokes by passers-by.

Meanwhile, the bridegroom with his friends, have their 'stag' party. An all-male drinking party which goes on late into the night, many a bridegroom has turned up for his wedding with more than apprehension for the minister making him shake.

In some parts of Scotland the bride's father throws small change to neighbourhood children as he and his daughter leave the house for the church. Called a 'Poor-oot' – pour out (of money) – it is another luck-bringer. The children at the Poor-oot often give the bride a horseshoe or black cat made out of cardboard – again for luck.

After the wedding ceremony, there is usually a reception with eating, drinking and dancing. If they are going on honeymoon, the bride and groom try to slip away before the party is over, though they are usually discovered and showered with confetti or rice. Confetti is also stuffed into the man's pockets and their suitcases so that when they reach their honeymoon hotel it is obvious that they are 'just married'. Couples who honeymoon at home are treated to 'apple-pie' beds – made by tucking the bedclothes in very tight – and rooms filled with balloons and confetti among other things. These and other customs, which have a very long history, ensure that the marriage will be a happy and fruitful one.

Whig Deriving from the word 'whiggamore', meaning horse drover, the name was originally applied to Scottish cattle rustlers and horse thieves, then to the *Covenanters* who marched on Edinburgh in 1648 and later, in the reign of James II, to those seeking to exclude the Duke of York from succession to the throne. The Whigs supported the Hanoverian succession and enjoyed a great deal of political power until the reign of George III, when they were superceded by the Tories. They regained their former political position in 1830 and thereafter were called 'Liberals'.

Whistle

> I sing of a Whistle, a Whistle of worth,
> I sing of a Whistle, the pride of the north,
> Was brought to the court of our good Scottish
>   king,
> And long with this Whistle all Scotland shall
>   ring.

The whistle which *Burns* wrote about has an interesting history. When Anne of Denmark came to Scotland with James VI she brought a very big man in her train. This Danish giant was a great drinker. At the start of every drinking session he laid a little ebony whistle on the table saying that whoever was the last to blow it, when everyone else was too drunk to do so, could have it as a prize. The Dane insisted that he had never been defeated anywhere in the world and challenged the Scots to live up to their reputation of being great drinkers. After three days and nights of hard drinking, the whistle was eventually won by Sir Robert Lowrie of Maxwelton who left the Dane under the table as he blew the whistle loud and shrill. Sir Robert's son, Walter, later lost the whistle to Walter Riddel of Glenriddel but on Friday, 16 October 1789 – the date which Burns commemorates in his poem – the whistle was once again contended for when the then Sir Robert Lowrie of Maxwelton tried to win it again for his family. Though he made a brave attempt, he lost it to a Mr Alexander Ferguson of Craigdarroch.

White Cockade A white rosette worn by the followers of *Bonnie Prince Charlie*. It was chosen as the emblem of the *Jacobites* in contrast to the black rosette worn by those loyal to the Hanoverian cause.

White Heather White heather is considered very lucky in Scotland. An old story tells that a pragmatic laird once went on a boar hunt. Unlike the other hunters, he would not take a good *luck* charm with him, saying he would rely on his good horse and his skill as a rider. The huntsmen rode off to hunt a boar in a nearby wood but the laird was separated from the other hunters and finally found himself on the outskirts of the wood at the edge of a steep cliff. Suddenly, the boar dashed out of the wood, frightening the horse so much that it reared and threw the laird over the cliff. He fell until his hand caught hold of a bush that was growing on the cliff face. He held on and called for help. The other hunters heard him and rescued him; but before he left the cliff, he sent one of his men down to get a piece of the plant that had saved his life. It was a white heather plant. He planted it in his garden and it grew into a very fine bush. From that day onwards every time the laird went past the plant he plucked a bit to put into his lapel for luck.

Whitsun One of the Scottish *Quarter-days*, it falls on 15 May. It takes its name from 'white' Sunday, a day of confirmation and *baptism* in the Church.

Witch In the past, due to *superstition* and ignorance, many an old country woman who knew *plant-lore*, a cripple or village idiot or even a man who seemed to be getting on a bit better than his neighbours, was accused of being a witch. Along with other European countries, Scotland suffered its share of witch trials and burnings and it has been estimated that from 1479 to 1722 17 000 people, including children, were tortured and executed as witches in Scotland.

Some witches are still remembered in Scotland today, among them Agnes Finnie who deprived twelve people of speech and Barbara Napier, a hawker who lived in the High Street, Edinburgh where she cast spells on 'gentlewomen'. Being accused of witchcraft was not the prerogative of the poor, however, for some 'gentlewomen', too, turn up on the pages of the trial books. One of those, Dame Euphane MacCalzean was accused in 1589 of trying to sink a ship which was carrying Anne of Denmark to marry James VI. The author of the book *Daemonologie*, James VI, who was a noted witch-hater, is said to have attended a trial where a man, despite the most cruel tortures, refused to confess to being a witch. James simply said that the man's refusal to confess was more evidence that the man was an agent of the *Devil* and had him burned.

Witchcraft is still practised in Scotland today. Having nothing to do with devil-worship, modern-day witches claim that they are members of an ancient religion connected with the female goddess Wicca. Treated with the tolerance which is often shown to people who are thought to be a little eccentric, witches meet at *Hallowe'en*, *Beltane* and on other days linked with the Celtic calendar where they celebrate in ways not vastly different from other folk.

Witches Flying Ointment A special ointment which witches rub on themselves so that they can fly. A recipe containing deadly nightshade, aconite, sweet flag, cinquefoil and smallage – plants which contain powerful hallucinogens – is mixed with bat's blood. This last ingredient works through 'sympathetic magic', for bats fly at night. The skin of certain toads, which contains Bufotenine, a powerful hallucinogen, is also sometimes included.

No one but a witch should attempt to make the ointment as the plants are highly poisonous and the wrong dosage could kill.

Bibliography

For readers wishing to follow up specific folklore topics, the following books are all readily available.

Music: Cowan, Edward J. (ed), *The People's Past,* Polygon, Edinburgh, 1980. Experts on folk culture contribute articles ranging from 'The Ballad, the Folk and the Oral Tradition' to 'Folk and Protest'.

Munro, Ailie, *The Folk-music Revival in Scotland,* Kahn and Averill, London, 1984. Includes musical notation reproducing the singing of the early revival ballad- and song-singers.

Folklore: Dorson, Richard M., *The British Folklorists,* Chicago University Press, London, 1968. This book covers the lives and work of the early antiquaries, folklorists and collectors, and contains many examples of the folklore they collected.

Chambers, Robert, *Traditions of Edinburgh,* Chambers, Edinburgh, 1824. Anecdotes of people and places in Edinburgh's Old Town, republished in 1980.

Agricultural and Fisher Life: Cameron, David Kerr, *The Ballad and the Plough,* Gollancz, London, 1978 and *Cornkister Days,* Gollancz, London, 1984 contain a wealth of information about life as it was lived in the old farmtouns of the north-east up until the beginning of the century.

Blair, Anna, *Croft and Creel,* Shepheard-Walwyn, London, 1987. A century of coastal memories, full of the personal experiences and ways of the fishing communities.

Stories: Williamson, Duncan, *A Thorn in the King's Foot,* Penguin, London, 1987 and *Tell me a story for Christmas,* Canongate, Edinburgh, 1987. Travellers' tales from a man whose repertoire includes approximately 3000 stories.

Burns: Ross Roy, G., *The Letters of Robert Burns,* Oxford, 1985. Two volumes of Burns's letters collected by J. De Lancey Ferguson and collated by the editor. The letters show the many faces of Burns: the exciseman, the farmer, the poet, the folk-song collector, the friend, the wooer.